Dear Mary,

I thought of you when someone said this was a good book for one who sometimes can't get to sleep.

I appreciate your continuing example and patience with me. May we always be friends!

love,
Merlene

BEDTIME STORIES
for GROWNUPS

BEDTIME STORIES *for* GROWNUPS

Elaine Cannon

BOOKCRAFT
Salt Lake City, Utah

Library of Congress Catalog Card Number: 88-71442

ISBN 0-88494-665-7

First Printing, 1988

Printed in the United States of America

*Yet a little sleep, a little slumber,
a little folding of the hands to sleep.*

—Proverbs 24:33

Contents

Preface

Bedtime stories for grown-ups?

Interesting idea. Everyone yearns for a moment of carefree, indulged childhood now and then, so what better time for an authentic adult to enjoy this than at bedtime?

Besides, most adults can't sleep when they fall into bed. Maybe some sleep in church, in front of the TV, at the opera, or at the piano recital of offspring, but not in bed.

This is a book to keep you contented *until you fall asleep*. It is a very grown-up book. It contains excerpts from the experts and quotes from the poets and philosophers, as well as opinions, perspectives, new findings, old jokes, recipes, lullabies, and a multitude of entertaining personal experiences. It has stories, too—bedtime stories—some of which are true and some are not, but all are perfect for a send-off into nighttime release.

Now, if you can talk someone into reading this book to you, a spouse or a grandchild, all the better. If that person has a monotone voice or a faltering style, you will be in sleep city before you can stutter "Sominex." But not before you have been pleasantly subdued by delightful and distracting bedtime reading material.

Becoming pleasantly subdued is the goal. We need pleasant thoughts to soothe the savage beast stirred up in us by a day in the marketplace or in the kitchen, keeping the home fires from destroying the place altogether. Clearly, it isn't the children who have problems at bedtime. It is the adults. When midnight comes, Oh that adults could turn into pumpkins past feeling.

But most can't.

Watching what happens when a grown-up hits the proverbial sack offers a laugh a second. You should be so lucky —watch and you might laugh yourself to sleep!

Some people climb into bed and cavort like the star in a TV mattress ad. Maybe you are one of these yourself, taking out all your frustration on the bedding. You punch the pillow, yank the covers, kick the mattress, and still can't drop off to sleep!

You rearrange your arms. What *do* other people do with their shoulders and their arms when they are trying to get comfortable in bed? If you try tucking your hands under your head, for example, only *they* go to sleep.

You work on relaxing your legs. You've already OD'd on calcium and quinine to calm thigh twitches, but to no avail.

You've taken your daily aspirin and you wait for soothing comfort—and wait and wait and wait . . .

You've counted the sheep and painted each picket of the fence they jump over.

You've inhaled deeply ten times and exhaled precisely the same way. You border on hyperventilation instead of sleep.

You've pretended you were ink on a blotter, an old psychological trick which some experts insist is the ultimate relaxing technique.

And I know one man who had a bout in the hospital and reverted to childhood in a flash of I.V. bottles and tubes. He couldn't sleep until his poor tired mother came to visit him. She's long gone now and the only way he gets sleepy is when a mother image is present.

Another fellow who can't sleep solves his problem by sliding up his sleeve and presenting his arm to be scratched.

Well, to each his own, but what do you do when you are alone in the Marriott?

Read *Bedtime Stories for Grownups*, of course. *Bedtime Stories for Grownups* is for people with problems they can't shake, tensions that tighten into muscle spasms, and vague aches that whisper of death.

One thing is certain: you need to turn off your mind. Just considering how to do that can keep some people awake. So how about reading something pleasant? You won't be sleeping—yet—but mind relaxation, body rest, and heart warming count for something.

This book is just lively and provocative and comforting enough to be a happy distraction from the wrestles, the battles, and the hangovers of daytime.

In the event that you are one of those rare grown-ups who, after praying, slide easily in between the sheets and confidently sprawl out flat with arms and legs akimbo, soon snoring in sweet sleep—in that event, beware! People can learn to hate you. Yet, even you can benefit from reading *Bedtime Stories for Grownups*: your dreams may become far more interesting.

This collection is so satisfying you probably will read it many other places besides in bed. Read it riding the mass transit system, waiting in the doctor's foyer, standing in the check-out line, by the poolside. Don't read it on the airplane, though, or your seatmate will snitch it when you doze off!

But do read *Bedtime Stories for Grownups*. Read on. And goodnight.

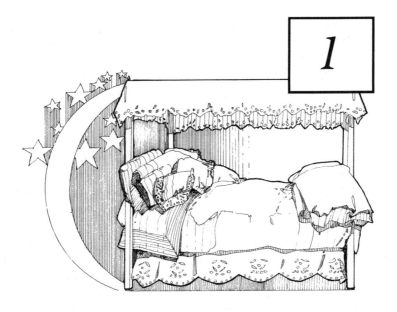

Come, Gentle Sleep

Come, gentle sleep! attend thy votary's prayer,
And, though death's image, to my couch repair;
How sweet, though lifeless, yet with life to lie,
And, without dying, O how sweet to die!
(Thomas Warton)

About that mattress wrestling I mentioned—I believe it is akin to ulcers. I vividly recall the response of O. Preston Robinson, who at the time was my boss at the *Deseret News*, when I told him that the doctor said I had ulcers and must keep to a strict diet.

Said Pres flatly, "Elaine, I don't care what the doctor says about dieting as a cure for ulcers. I have learned that ulcers come not because of what you are eating but because of what is eating you!"

So it is with tossing and turning in bed.

Peace. That's what we need. The destroying angels about our house, notwithstanding. Finding peace—as differentiated from quiet—brings pleasant thoughts, a softened heart, gentle sleep.

And subdued ulcers, maybe.

One way of spelling peace is r-e-c-o-n-c-i-l-i-a-t-i-o-n. It can be a smart move to try to reconcile problems before going to bed—reconcile ideas waging war in the brain; religious principles with political or social impositions; life's seasons with life's situations. Reconciliation with people, however, fosters personal peace and gentle sleep probably more than anything else.

The irate father said to his errant son:

"Son, did you hear the last thing I said to you?"

"I sure hope so," answered the sour youth.

Typical, perhaps, but not hopeless. Could be a situation to keep you awake nights, though. Or start your own version of the prodigal.

I know one ward where two men live who haven't spoken to each other in fifteen years. Each Sunday they faithfully participate in the same priesthood quorum meeting. They just don't speak to each other. It might not be so serious if they didn't happen to be father and son!

Now, that is enough to disturb one's rest pattern.

A young man had been missing from home for three days —he and his motorcycle and his black leather jacket. Where was he? Was he alive or dead? Why hadn't he called home? Yes, he'd been in trouble, but if only he'd come home all would be forgiven. If only . . . if only . . . if only . . .

I was visiting in this affluent home during this time of anguish over a missing teenage son. The parents were professionals, each successful in a field related to medicine. There were tears, prayers, promises, questions, pain, and even accusations as they waited for word from the police department.

At last the doorbell rang and the mother hurried to answer. A policeman was standing at the door. He informed the mother that her boy had been found and picked up by another police officer. By then, the father had come to the door, just in time to see the son arrive.

The black leather jacket was ripped. The young man's eyes were swollen, his face puffy, and his hands scratched and scraped. His head was cut. His clothes filthy. It was not a pleasant sight if you were looking for perfection, but if you were looking for a son he looked wonderful anyway! At least, that's how I felt.

The parents immediately turned into disciplinarians. "Where have you been?" they shouted together at the bedraggled, unhappy boy. Then they piled a barrage of accusative questions upon him. All the worry and caring the parents felt *before* he returned had disappeared.

There was not a word about welcome home or thanks to God. No enveloping arms. No tears of joy.

All we heard was the firm reminder that if that young man was to live in that house he'd have to keep the household rules or there would be worse problems.

Young shoulders sagged. The officer of the law stiffened and turned. A prodigal had been returned, but one wondered how long he'd stay, how much his life would change.

3

Somebody has to be the peacemaker in such a situation, and it might need to be the parents. Some parents don't realize that they are old enough to know better.

I have come to believe that the story of the prodigal son is the supportive scripture behind the great secrets of personal peace and nightly slumber. It is about reconciliation, which is about Christlike love. The biblical account of the prodigal son is a good bedtime story for grown-ups.

Most of today's prodigals aren't seeking their fortune when they bolt the home fires. They have it so easy at home —what with comfortable housing, trendy clothing, stacks of sports equipment, and electronic toys ad nauseum.

Freedom is what today's prodigals are after. Not the flag-waving kind, but the kind that spares their little psyches from the restrictions of family rules. These household standards can be the ties that not only bind but also gag, as Erma Bombeck so aptly puts it.

Reconciliation becomes a valuable ideal to most parents with such a sleep-stealing problem. After all, they've given the best years of their lives and most of their capital to their offspring.

To me, the most intriguing character in the biblical parable is the father, not the prodigal. That magnificent, forgiving father; that master of reconciliation. What an inspiration! Imagine, rushing out to meet that disaffected, selfish, sinning son. And with fatted calf and jewelry, too.

Granted, one doesn't just recall only the father's response. Something needs to be said about the repentant son who mustered the courage to go home and face the music. But it is the father who serves the example in the scriptural story.

This parable is good bedtime reading for grown-ups largely because of the attitude and actions of the father.

You see, the father did not wait proudly until his wayward son walked in the door, head hanging low as he begged forgiveness. That father didn't stand his "rightful ground" as an authority figure until that son had walked right up to him, groveling and suffering and mortified, expecting a lecture on the theme, "I told you so!"

Rather, as soon as the father noted that the prodigal was coming home, though he was yet a great way off, the father ran to meet him. Ran!

There followed a celebration of joy. No doubt about it, family love was stronger than human frailty. Forgiveness was a part of that family's life-style. You can be sure both Father and son—to say nothing of Mother—had their first good night's sleep in a long time. The next day is time enough for a rehearsal of rules.

I was a small child riding in the back seat as my mother drove my grandmother to another county to see her long-estranged brother. The miles to travel allowed plenty of time for yet another rehash of the old problem. The years between the last visit of brother with sister had been painful indeed. It was a matter of inheritance. The brother had taken control of the parents' estate and she was cheated out, being a "mere woman." Well, Grandmother was also a struggling widow in a time when social security and retirement programs weren't the norm.

Anyway, Grandmother was angry. I had never seen her like this and it was shocking to me, so I was paying close attention.

I was at the age where I believed in Red Queens, and trolls, ogres, and giants at the top of bean stalks, wicked step-mothers, and witches with poisoned apples. I was anxious to see my grandmother's brother. I'd never seen a real live ogre before.

The time passed and the wisdom of my Spirit-directed mother was calming and healing. Blood was thicker than water. Obedience to gospel principles brought their own reward—at least, a good night's sleep. Grandmother was calmed at last.

When the car stopped at last, I looked at the ordinary farmhouse with its screened porch and whirling sprinkler. There was no moat, no dragon—just an ordinary man coming down the steps in dark pants and a white shirt. His suspenders fell free of his shoulders to hang below his thick waist. His shirt sleeves were folded over black elastic garters around his large biceps. He was no ogre. He was a raw-faced, red-necked, balding, brawny farmer who had dressed in his Sunday best for the Reconciliation.

Grandmother was dressed up, too. She was wearing her brooch as well as her pearls. After so many years of separation, first impressions were important.

She got out of the car with only slight hesitation and started up the walk. She, who had suffered and angered long, was now determined to do what was best and conducive to peace.

She pressed toward the mark. He rushed down the steps to greet her, arms outstretched. And as he enveloped her in his arms, I heard her muffled cry of joy, "Oh, Ez!"

"Eva!"

Details didn't matter. Love did. In the wake of tears of reunion, it was clear that "making up" was wonderful. Some things simply are more important than others, after all.

In the fine movie *Papillon*—with Steve McQueen as Henri Charriere—on whose book the movie is based—there is a line worth remembering. There had been trouble between friends, and one, Degas, is discussing the matter with a third party.

"Will you blame him?" the man asked Degas.

"Blame," replied Degas, "is for God and children."

Who among us is spiritually mature enough for ready sleep?

Sooner or later, most of us learn how to handle crises properly. It is often the shallow offenses that do us in, that keep us awake nights. They try our stamina as well as our character.

Lying in bed counting the offenses we've suffered that day is not a lot worse than counting people we "ought" to forgive for such offenses. This only serves to remind us of injustices—real or imagined.

One distinguished citizen of our community says he's an absolute genius in the wee hours of the morning. He composes exquisite letters that burn and shame while listing the wrongs of this leader or that church procedure. He doesn't send them. All that comes of such activity is a restless soul and crumpled bed linens and punched pillows.

We're not talking about salvation of the soul here, we're talking about being able to sleep at night, though the two may have much in common.

It may help some to remember that there is a whole city or church congregation out there in the darkness who manage to snore away without writing those phantom letters to the editor, the city fathers, or church leaders!

Reconciliation is with self, then. If there isn't anything we can personally do about it, forget it. Roll over and go to sleep.

Though it is important to heal the hurts that we think we don't deserve, that we have caused, or that are simply not what we had counted on as part of life's relentless testing, it is wise to understand that we can't turn every poke at our pride or our peace into a crisis requiring forgiveness before we can sleep. Sometimes it is better to swallow annoyances with a cup of warm milk. A complicated world is forever imposing such sleep-stealers upon us. Leave for the deeper assaults the dramatics of full-scale reconciling and forgiving. I agree with Lewis B. Smedes, author of *Forgive and Forget* (Pocket Books of New York), who says that ''wholesale forgiving is too much for anybody.'' Except for God, I'd add. Maybe forgetting is a good part of reconciliation and peace.

Sleep it off. You'll feel better in the morning.

Peace doesn't come by hunting frantically for it like a coin lost under kitchen appliances. It comes from yielding to the steps it takes to bring it about in one's mind and heart. Or heart and then mind. Sometimes the heart may feel what the mind doesn't understand yet.

There is another side to this coin, though. It is the side of the person who is forgiven for something he didn't know he'd done.

For example, there is a woman who is constantly—and elaborately—forgiving her husband for whatever annoying thing he has just done. Like not tossing his soiled socks into the laundry hamper. This lady is forever celebrating Martyr's Day: ''Harry, I forgive you for not putting your dirty socks in the laundry. As long as I have to wash your socks, I can just as well bend over and pick them up, too. That's why I was born. Yes, I forgive you, Harry. Don't worry a thing about it, Harry.''

Harry doesn't. And the maddening part is that Harry is the first to sleep at night, and the last to awaken in the morning.

Remember the old *New Yorker* cartoon that shows the husband coming in drunk and being chastised by the irate wife in her frumpy, nighttime getup. She really lets him have it. A true lecture, colorful and abusive.

And that cool drunk faces his life with her by saying: "Never mind, Snookums. To err is human, to forgive is divine."

So why do we consider this subject at all?

Isn't it because happiness is what peace brings? Each day is an attempt at cleaning up our act, reconciling our unpleasantness, overcoming the hurts—or simply silencing the pain, easing the stress, repenting, and making restitution if we can —considering what is "eating us," and deciding whether it matters all that much.

Norman Vincent Peale has written the following fine lines:

> Everybody really knows what to do to have his life filled with joy. What is it? Quit hating people; start loving them. Quit being mad at people; start liking them. Quit doing wrong, quit being filled with fear. Quit thinking about yourself and go out and do something for other people. Everybody knows what you have to do to be happy. But the wisdom of the test lies in the final word, "If ye know these things, happy are ye if ye do them." (*Treasure Chest*, p. 20.)

George Albert Smith was a young Utah National Guardsman when he learned the value of reconciliation. He was being considered for some kind of special leadership assignment or personal award, when a man he thought was his friend started damaging rumors about him.

George lost the recognition because of this cruel act. He felt he was entitled to it and that he had been cheated out of it. His heart filled with hurt and anger toward his former friend. His life became miserable. The more he thought about the disappointing situation, the more it ballooned in importance and destroyed his peace.

His bitterness escalated to the point where he felt uncomfortable taking the sacrament of the Lord's Supper. He began to pray about it. He desired some kind of revenge, but he was a disciple of Christ and knew that such action was not in keeping with such high ideals. Although he did nothing overtly to destroy the guilty man, the hurt still rankled his soul. Time passed, and George finally grasped the perspective that the incident hadn't seemed to affect his former friend. He, George Albert Smith, was wronging only himself with the burden of hate he carried.

Reconciliation was the only answer. Get it off his chest and be done with it. Life was about more than this.

He went to the place of business of the man who had spread the damaging falsehoods. When the man saw George Albert coming, he automatically raised his arm in a kind of mock shield over his face. He thought he was in for a beating.

George Albert had prepared himself for the occasion through fervent prayer. By the time he had courageously made the attempt to confront his enemy, he was mollified and full of the Spirit. His voice was gentle and his manner humble. He considered himself at fault for giving in to hate and anger. He expressed this to his friend, who lowered his arm, bowed his head, and listened quietly as George Albert said, "I want you to forgive me for the anger I have felt in these past weeks, for the way I have been hating."

"George Albert, you have no need for forgiveness. It is I who need forgiveness from you."

Because of Smith's spiritual maturity and his willingness to reconcile past problems in favor of peace, the enemy was subdued. Friendship was possible again.

Of such is a man of God made.

Sometimes sleep fails to come because we're lonely. This word to widows and widowers, to the never married, the friendless, the angry-hearted who haven't reconciled their differences with others: Even if we can't be together with a friend or loved one, if we are reconciled in heart, reaching toward each other with caring spirits, distance and circumstance have little power to destroy peace and contentment.

Anwar-I-Suheili expressed the same thought in this way: "Am I united with my friend in heart, what matters if our place be wide apart?"

To be reconciled with God makes it easier to be reconciled with people. Poet-teacher George Herbert, who lived in the seventeenth century, wrote a poem called *The Pulley* which rings true to me.

When God at first made man,
Having a glass of blessings standing by;
Let us, (said he) pour on him all we can:
Let the world's riches, which dispersed lie,
Contract into a span.

So strength first made a way;
Then beauty flowed, then wisdom, honour, pleasure: . . .
Perceiving that alone of all His treasure
Rest [peace] in the bottom lay.

For if I should (said He)
Bestow this jewel also on My creature,
He would adore My gifts instead of Me,
And rest in Nature, not the God of Nature.
So both should losers be.

Yet let him keep the rest,
But keep them with repining restlessness:
Let him be rich and weary, that at least,
If goodness lead him not, yet weariness
May toss him to My breast.

(George Herbert, *Masterpieces of Religious Verse* [Harper and Row: New York and Evanston, 1948], pp. 266–67.)

People today often leap from one guru to another, pursue earthly lusts, entertain sophistries of the mind, engage in disciplines for muscles, give in to appetites and addictions, and then, at last, must turn to God or go under in exhaustion and despair.

The Book of Mormon lends another perspective. It is from Helaman 12:3: "And thus we see that except the Lord doth chasten his people with many afflictions, yea, except he doth visit them with death and with terror, and with famine and with all manner of pestilence, they will not remember him."

Time after time, the history of mankind has proven this to be so.

Some years ago, David Lawrence McKay shared a story about his grandchild at bedtime. Grandpa was given the privilege of helping with prayers. The three-year-old knelt at Lawrence's knee and began the precious ritual. When the simple, earnest prayer was over, the child remained kneeling and silent. Unusual! Most scramble into life again with demands for stuffed toys, bedtime stories, drinks of water, and yet another goodnight kiss. Not this one. The silence persisted until Grandpa questioned why the child didn't pop into bed.

"Sh-h-h, Grandfather. I am listening!"

Ah-ah! And shouldn't listening be part of all communication? Particularly with Heavenly Father. Such lessons the little ones can teach.

Let's go back again to the story of the prodigal. It seems to be an especially insightful scripture as to the great secret of personal peace. And a good night's rest, as well. The first two great commandments of God are based on such reconciliation as we've been describing.

Consider again the son who "came to himself" and who said, "I will arise and go to my father. . . . " Consider the father, who, seeing the son when he was yet a great way off, felt overcome with compassion and "ran, and fell on his neck, and kissed him."

Reunion. Reconciliation. Restoration. Wholeness. Reciprocal communication. Peace.

Peace usually begins at home and advances to reconciliation with God. But the other way around works just as well. Find peace with God and one can't rest until wrongs are righted at home. Then that place becomes a heaven on earth, and all who sit at the table are as if at the Lord's supper.

Here are a few nostalgic lines to consider:

I knew by the smoke, that so gracefully curl'd
Above the green elms, that a cottage was near,
And I said, "If there's peace to be found in the world,
A heart that was humble might hope for it here!"

That's Thomas Moore, a master at saying what we may feel on a given subject. Adelaide Ann Procter in *Per Pacem and Lucem* penned these lines:

Joy is like the restless day; but peace divine
Like quiet night;
Lead me, O Lord, till perfect day shall shine
Through Peace to Light.

Brief thoughts at bedtime are usually better than lengthy treatises that the mind is too tired to handle. Often the problem with being wide awake when one is supposed to be sound asleep is that one is too tired to think rationally, but not too tired to stay awake.

Short of hypnosis, reading a selection of quotations can work wonders with restlessness.

The following is credited to Henry Van Dyke and is a good benediction before sleep:

To be glad of life because it gives you the chance to love and to work and to play and to look up at the stars, to be satisfied with your possessions but not contented with yourself until you have made the best of them, to despise nothing in the world except falsehood and meanness and to fear nothing except cowardice, to be governed by your admirations rather than by your disgusts, to covet nothing that is your neighbor's except his kindness of heart and gentleness of manners, to think seldom of your enemies, often of your friends, and every day of Christ, and to spend as much time as you can with body and spirit, in God's out of doors, these are little guideposts on the footpath to peace.

Wonderful! Wonderful! Blessed are the peacemakers.

Mary Englebert designed a greeting card with unusual appeal. It is illustrated with animals and charming children under a star-filled sky, rollicking together among trumpets, ribbon streamers, hoops, and hugs. The message is from Chekhov:

> We shall find peace.
> We shall hear the angels.
> We shall see the sky sparkling with diamonds.

And on such a day, who will want to go to sleep?

After all, sometimes staying awake has its own reward.

As a parting thought about trying to sleep, how about just lying there feeling peaceful—counting blessings instead of sheep or problems?

When else, these days, but in the still of the night, is there privacy enough to take out old memories and wallow in a certain success, dream again of a lost romance, recall a spiritual experience, live again a childhood day, remember a lesson learned or a kindness done.

There is value in being alone with one's thoughts while the rest of the world sleeps.

So . . . if gentle sleep doesn't come at once . . . who cares about that for one wonderful night!

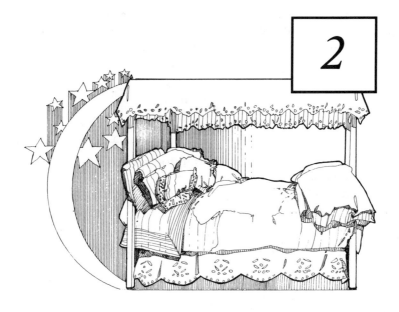

Sweet Dreams

On I-15 going south from Salt Lake City, Utah, is a billboard featuring Russell's ice cream. The screamer represents my philosophy exactly: "Life is short. Eat dessert first!"

Here's another angle: if you long for sweet dreams, eat dessert last—as a bedtime snack.

It may sound decadent and self-indulging. But that's the general idea. It's what soothes a stressed soul.

I can't guarantee that this method will induce peaceful rest. In fact, for many of us nightmares are more likely. Or refrigerator raids. Some gourmet types may find themselves dragging the food processor out of storage amid a flurry of eggs, almond paste, and melted chocolate. At 2:00 A.M., too.

So read on at your own risk; but remember, just desserts can make trying to get to sleep an adventure in sweet dreams.

Years ago, over a bowl of creamy seafood bisque at the Marvin O. Ashton home, Bishop Ashton informed me that it was all right to give guests soup if you served them a "roaring homemade dessert" as well.

"Take my wife's toffee," said Bishop Ashton. "Now, *that* is what I call a roaring dessert." He reached for the silver compote perilously piled with crunchy toffee—courtesy of Rae Jeremy Ashton—and passed it to me to prove a point.

I took the toffee and the counsel.

When the State Dairy Association asked me to do a celebrity cookbook, I included Mrs. Ashton's bisque. She also shared her toffee recipe and priceless tips for unfailing success.

Rae claimed that a good candy maker has a candy pan which is not used for cooking anything but candy: a precaution that protects against "foreign flavors" tainting the delicate sweet mix. The pan should be wide, deep, and heavy. Never mind how used it looks. A candy pan that looks used is owned by an experienced candy maker, and the product leaves a grown man crying for more, or dreaming about it in his sleep.

I heard somebody say that "a dieter is thick and tired of it." Even so, dieters will fight to lick such a pan when this candy is poured out to cool. There is plenty for licking, too, because Rae said not to scrape the pan when the candy is poured out to cool or it might turn to sugar.

Another secret of making candy is to use only quality ingredients, such as sweet butter, thick cream, and fresh nuts broken into sizeable chunks you can sink your teeth into.

One caution Mrs. Ashton shared that I've never forgotten is that you should always stir up the full recipe for toffee. Half a batch is never enough. The candy is that good! On the other hand, if you double the recipe you may be disappointed. Toffee must cook fast, and too much sugar in the pan at one time may take too long to dissolve, disappointing both the cook and the candy eater.

And if you aren't about asleep by now, try settling down with a piece of Rae Ashton's Best Ever Toffee. Here's the recipe. Watch out, Mrs. See's!

Rae Ashton's Best Ever Toffee

1 lb sweet cream butter
2 cups white sugar
⅓ cup water
2 cups toasted almonds
½ tsp real vanilla

Butter cookie sheet and cover with coarsely chopped nuts. In the candy pan, add all remaining ingredients except vanilla. Bring to a boil, stirring constantly until sugar is dissolved and mix begins to change color slightly. Cook without stirring until candy becomes toffee-colored. If you use a candy thermometer, insert one at this point and cook until it reads 280° at sea level. Add vanilla. Lift pan gently and shake around to mix in vanilla. Pour over nuts. Set pan on cooling rack and candy will cool faster.

This is an easy, quickly made treat. You'll be asleep before you know it.

If a person has Las Vegas roots and is a clean-living young man, like Milt Sharp, eating at midnight is the name of the game. Like cherry pie at bedtime, that is really cool comfort and promises sound sleep.

When it comes to cherry pie at bedtime, Milt says he'll take the pie filling any way at all—filling with more cherries than sauce or skimping on the cherries and heavy on the sauce. Less sauce makes less mess though, if you eat it in bed!

Either way, a squeeze of lemon and a drop of almond flavoring dolls up canned cherry pie filling just right.

Milt travels a great deal for his profession in continuing education, and he says that cherry pie is one thing you can usually get any hour of the day from room service. There are advantages to liking cherry pie!

It makes all the difference if a fellow can choose the pie crust. Some ladies serve cardboard crust and call it pie, but according to Milt it is simply that—cardboard. Flaky, tender crust with the bottom layer cooked clear through are his specifications. Here is Milt's favorite method:

Pie Crust

2 cups all-purpose flour
½ tsp salt
1 cup real butter
1 T vinegar
2 T cold water

In a mixing bowl combine flour and salt. Cut butter into flour until crumbly. Sprinkle with vinegar and water. Lightly mix until dough forms together in a ball. Set in a cool place for fifteen minutes. Roll, fill, bake, and eat! Or simply form into little tartlets, bake at 400° for ten minutes, and spoon in filling.

Men who can't sleep make wonderful cooks. Just watch them whirl eggs into something delightful—scrambled eggs at midnight, maybe—though dessert-type food promises the sweetest of dreams.

You may think you have died and gone to heaven if you pacify your sleeplessness with a private serving of thin, eggy crepes or thick, fluffy hotcakes drizzled with boysenberry syrup or apricot preserves—spun with melted butter.

My brother Lowell learned to cook in France, and he can make a midnight breakfast so delicious it could be labeled dessert.

At our family cabin on Hebgen Lake in Montana's Big Sky Country, Lowell would work wonders on the antique, black, coal stove. He'd whiz about flipping the hotcakes, warming the ham, simmering the homemade maple syrup, hashing the cottage potatoes, while watching thick slices of Mother's bread toasting. Besides this, he'd cook the trout just so—if we were lucky enough to have caught some. Eggs and omelettes were made according to order—even at the last moment.

Lowell would cook these up in the morning or at midnight or whenever!

However, for a romantic push into dreamland, Lowell recommends French Puff Pancake for two. This recipe allows time for the cook and his companion to indulge in precious talk while the Puff puffs. Twenty minutes, give or take a little, and your impressive, sky-high puff will be ready.

Midnight Puff

3 T real butter
3 eggs
½ cup milk
dash of salt
1 T sugar
½ cup flour

In 450° oven, melt and brown butter in a two-quart casserole or soufflé dish. Meanwhile, break eggs into a blender (or whip with a hand beater). Whip for one minute. Add milk, salt, sugar, and flour. Blend for another minute. Pour batter in hot butter. Bake for about twenty minutes without opening the oven for the first fifteen minutes. Serve at once.

At midnight, soup is often taken as a tonic for sleep. But as part of a collection of bedtime desserts, there is only one soup that qualifies to be included. That's borscht.

Dr. Homer Ellsworth has delivered thousands of babies, meanwhile keeping his "ladies" laughing with apropos humor. During his long career as an obstetrician, Dr. Ellsworth has collected an endless supply of material for laughs. He also has Chef Girard's recipe for borscht—that rare dish so popular with patrons during the Hotel Utah's golden era.

Homer's parting shot to anyone making this borscht is: "Unless you make it good, don't blame it on Chef Girard."

Homer makes it "good." Here's how:

Chef Girard's Borscht

1 qt beet juice or canned beets
2 cups chicken stock
1 tsp Accent
2 tsp fresh lemon juice
2 T cornstarch
2 cups sour cream
4 egg yolks

Whip beet juice or canned beets thoroughly in blender. Add chicken stock, Accent, and lemon juice. Bring to a boil. Dissolve cornstarch in a little cold water. Stir into hot soup. Boil slowly for five minutes. Meanwhile, combine sour cream with beaten egg yolks. Pour one cup hot soup into the egg mixture. Then return all ingredients to the pot of soup and stir well. Heat well but do *not* boil. Serve with a garnish of unsweetened whipped cream, a bit of grated hard-boiled egg, a parsley sprig, or a thin lemon slice. You choose. It's so good you can even eat it plain.

This recipe serves eight. Unless you are having a slumber party, you may want to make only half a recipe's worth.

However, if you do make it all, it will taste just as pleasing tomorrow night.

High in the Wasatch mountains, Debbie Fields has a smashing estate. It is said to have thirteen bathrooms. That comes from selling a lot of cookies!

I think every young girl should be taught to make a proper chocolate chip cookie. That instruction should come before white sauce, which is what I learned first in my cooking class in junior high.

If there is anything that most men enjoy at any hour of the day, but especially as a preface for sweet sleep, it is a good chocolate chip cookie. Some say boy babies are weaned to chocolate chip cookies. Their only bias seems to be that the cookie must be three-fourths chocolate chips and one-fourth whatever that stuff is that holds them into a cookie shape.

When the tiny kisses were packaged for the convenience of the housewife and all her cookie-eating family, we knew that the Depression was over. Toll House cookies made at home—wow! Little chocolate morsels to snack on late at night changed everybody's life. You can try substituting apple slices, wheat nuggets, or carrot strips—but chocolate is where the comfort is.

There are a lot of great chocolate chip cookie recipes around. Some use oatmeal as a filler. Some stress dark chocolate bits and no nuts. Some use hunks of milk-dipping chocolate. Some, heaven forbid, mix in raisins.

Some people claim to have Mrs. Fields's original recipe. Maybe they do, but Mrs. Fields says that her recipe is patented and protected. It's her personal gold mine.

Mrs. Fields and her cookies are something to dream about, but in case you are out of chocolate chip cookies and the store is closed when you need them to get to sleep, you might like to have this excellent recipe handy. It isn't Debbie Fields's, but it's close. And the yield is dreamy. They are Doug Sorensen's favorite.

21

A Chocolate Chip Cookie to Dream On

2 ½ cups flour
½ tsp salt
1 tsp baking soda
1 pinch nutmeg
1 cup shortening
¾ cup brown sugar
¼ cup white sugar
2 eggs
2 T water
1 tsp vanilla
chocolate chips
nuts (optional)

Sift together flour, salt, baking soda, and nutmeg. [The good cook puts in a pinch of nutmeg when cooking for loved ones.] Set aside.

Cream the shortening well, at least half of which is real butter. Add sugars and blend well. Add eggs and water. Blend until fluffy. Mix in dry ingredients. Flavor with vanilla. [Again, it's a matter of choice whether to use real butter and real vanilla, and if you can't taste the difference between the real and the imitation, it's too bad. Better to forget the cookies and turn over and go to sleep hungry!]

Nuts are optional, but if you do use them they go in at this point with the package of chocolate chips. Spoon batter onto greased cookie sheets and bake in a preheated oven at 350° for ten to twelve minutes or until lightly brown. You may want to bake one cookie first to test your oven. "An overdone chocolate chip cookie is a blight on mankind," says Elder Robert L. Backman, whose favorite dessert at Deseret Gym board meetings is an assortment of cookies. Fitness specialist Backman claims that cookies saved in a doggie bag make a special bedtime treat with a glass of milk.

Our daughter, who understands about men and chocolate, was making a pecan pie for a party. She tossed in some chocolate chips with the pecans and had a true hit of a dessert, according to her husband, Richard Metcalf. Just imagine, the last piece of pecan pie at bedtime. Oh, you'll go all over the world in your dreams.

While serving as the Young Women general president, I had the privilege of traveling with President and Sister Kimball on many occasions. On one trip I came prepared with several rolls of homemade fudge. I've found that Church leaders, travel agents, and security men alike need a touch of home on a long jaunt. I shared a bit of fudge with President Kimball's personal security man one day. He was delighted, but the next day he came asking for more . . . almost sheepishly, but with a convincing explanation. It seems he had shared his piece with President Kimball. Was there any more, by chance? Fortunately there was, but not enough to wholly satisfy that gentle spiritual giant of a small-statured man, who had a craving for chocolate in rice country!

Later I remedied that.

President Kimball was about to celebrate his eightieth birthday. I asked the members of the general board of the Young Women to join me in a wonderful surprise. We cooked over eighty pounds of fudge and molded it into foil-wrapped logs. I had the display department at ZCMI custom make a handsome, lidded lucite box, 18″ square and 24″ high. We filled the box with the fudge, put the lid on the box, and topped it with an enormous festive bow. On the big day we presented it to President Kimball. When we had sung "Happy birthday dear President Kimball!" and made the presentation of fudge, he laughed and said: "My goodness, I wasn't aware that we had asked for two-year supply of fudge!" But he loved it!

The cooks were my counselors, Arlene Darger and Norma B. Smith, and Linda Palmer, Mona Layton, Winnifred C. Jardine, Janet Palmer, Grethe B. Peterson, Kay Warner, Mary Briggs, Jeanene Stringham, Patricia Weed, Janyce Fisher, Sharon Lewis, Margery S. Cannon, and Sue C. Smith.

The recipe we used is a family favorite. I once made this much fudge by myself for a daughter's wedding. People loved slicing off their own hunk on a decorative cutting board.

Cousin Winnifred Jardine worked out the no-fail method. I had it printed on a card to hand out along with the programs for one of my *Seminar for Sallies and Sams* that we held for twenty years as a back-to-school promotional event for the teenagers of Utah-and-beyond. This best-ever, made-from-scratch fudge recipe is as follows:

Best-Ever Fudge

> 1 ¾ cups milk
> dash of salt
> 4 squares unsweetened chocolate, grated
> 4 cups sugar
> 2 T butter
> 2 tsp real vanilla

Scald milk with salt. Stir in chocolate until it completely melts. Gradually add sugar, stirring constantly until dissolved.

Wash down the sides of the pan with a wet pastry brush. Cover the pan for one minute. Uncover and cook until the candy reaches the firm ball stage. Pour into *buttered* dripper pan with butter added on top of the hot candy. Cool. Add vanilla and beat until it becomes creamy fudge.

No doubt about it, when it comes to chocolate, most men are adamant. Take Stan Darger, for example. This bank executive has lost pounds, regained his good health, and given red meat the good-bye song. But chocolate—a grown man doesn't want to live without a little chocolate now and then.

The best way to bid adieu to the hassles of the world and to enter the twilight time of sleep is with double chocolate brownies.

That's according to Stan, who is an absolute chocolate connoisseur. Stan was nurtured on chocolate-frosted dough-nuts from the old United Grocery in Salt Lake City, Utah. He graduated to chocolate doughnuts à la mode at the old College Inn by the University of Utah. Life moves on and so does Stan. Now he enjoys a good brownie at bedtime, especially when vacationing.

This is the recipe he likes:

Double Trouble Brownies for Bedtime

4 eggs
2 cups white sugar
1 square butter or margarine
3 squares semisweet chocolate
½ cup milk
1 ¼ cup flour
½ tsp salt
1 tsp real vanilla
package of chocolate chips
nuts (optional)

Beat eggs until fluffy. Continue beating while gradually adding sugar. Meanwhile, melt butter or margarine and choc-olate together. Cool with milk. Add to egg mixture. Beat well. Sift together flour and salt. Fold into egg mixture. Stir in vanilla. Nuts are optional, but the chocolate chips are added at this time. Grease and flour an oblong cake or dripper pan. Bake in a preheated oven at 350° for about forty minutes. Remove from the oven and sprinkle immediately with sifted powdered sugar. Eat at once or someone else will—especially if you wait until the brownies are cool and frosted!

Some people are confirmed refrigerator-robbers. They can't sleep until they've checked out the goodies in cold storage. English trifle can often be built from whatever fruit and custard the nonsleeper can find on hand.

My recipe for trifle is precious to me, partly because it tastes so good any hour of the day, and partly because of the man who made it for me in London.

A first visit to England or Europe is almost more exciting than a person can imagine. The people, the food, the sheer impact of the passage of time, the witness of civilization's history, and the awareness of one's own naivete is heightened when one sees it all through the perspective of a native cook.

Being a guest in the British Mission home many years ago, the first time I crossed the Atlantic, was like that for me. I met Jack, the mission's cook, who let me work alongside him a time or two in his quaint kitchen. That's where I learned about English trifle—one takes a bit of this and a tad of that and "Cheerio! Dessert!" explained Jack.

Jack is long gone now, but his recipe lingers on in my life. Try it at bedtime and you may dream about a tour of Britain's Lake Country, or a dinner with Di and Charles.

Authentic English Trifle

> variety of sponge or pound cake
> flavored gelatin
> bananas
> custard
> berries
> peaches (sliced)
> nuts
> whipped cream

To make an authentic English trifle use your loveliest clear glass bowl and layer it with a colorful variety of sponge or pound cake—moistened with juice or flavored gelatin—

bananas, custard, berries, sliced peaches, nuts, and dollops of whipped cream. Refrigerate for an hour or two, at least, before eating in bed.

You have to plan ahead for this goodnight goodie. But it is worth it, and can make staying awake until you are sleepy so much more pleasant.

On one trip abroad, T. Upton and Rhoda Ramsey worked out travel arrangements to squeeze in some time for their individual pursuits. While Rhoda checked out historical real estate, Uppy went to cooking school.

Uppy is now a favorite chef, cooking class instructor, food columnist, and charming host with rare dishes to serve. You should be so lucky as to stay awake dreaming about Uppy's flan, torte, or pots de crème.

Better still, get out of bed and make some on your own. Here's a choice recipe for authentic European pots de crème.

Upton Ramsey's Pots de Crème

> 6 oz semisweet chocolate
> 1 ¼ cups cream or half-and-half
> 2 egg yolks
> dash of salt

In saucepan, combine chocolate and cream. Stir over low heat until creamy and smooth. Beat egg yolks with salt until light and can form a ribbon. Gradually stir egg mixture into hot chocolate. Spoon into pots. Cover, and chill three hours. Makes six portions.

Cecilia Ludwig was trained to cook in some of the royal households of Europe. She's the author of a new cookbook called *Royal Dining*. For many years she owned a restaurant in

Leeds, Utah, where she served guests the kind of food that left them dreaming in the daytime as well as at night.

Cecilia shared a tip about pots de creme. She suggests spooning the mix into paper-lined muffin tins and popping them in the freezer. When the creme is frozen, the muffin-sized servings may be stored in the muffin liners and the tins returned to the cupboard for further use. When you want one for a bedtime send-off, you merely need to take it from the freezer, peel off the muffin paper, and slip the creme into a serving dish. Wonderful!

Bill Ross works hard as the force behind Beta Sigma Phi, headquartered in Kansas City, Missouri. Bill's father founded this women's organization during the Depression to help women progress and grow through group study in those difficult times.

Now as much as Bill loves the members of Beta Sigma Phi —he doesn't draw the line with women cooks, since he knows that some men have the gift of gourmet cooking. Bill knows about gourmet food. He is a thoughtful host, which is an art in itself, and when I used to work for him and would go to Kansas City for meetings, I was served the finest food Kansas City had to offer.

The best dessert I've ever eaten (that wasn't chocolate) was at the River Club in Kansas City. Mr. Ross introduced me to the chef and club manager, David Phyffe, who had made it especially for me. He shared his recipe knowing full well I wouldn't open a restaurant across the street from his establishment.

Whip up this lemon soufflé at bedtime and you won't care whether you go to sleep or not. It's inches high, fragile and pale, fluffy and gently sweet. It is just tart enough to please. It is so satisfying that it just might lull you drowsy.

Cold Lemon Soufflé

1 qt heavy cream, whipped firm
8 egg yolks beaten until thick and lemon-colored
1 lb of fine granulated sugar
juice and zest of 3 lemons
2 cups of water
raspberries
1 T honey

Cook sugar with water until it makes a heavy syrup (it should spin off a spoon about like commercial pancake syrup). Add lemon juice to egg yolks in double boiler, beating constantly. Cook until mixture is thick like custard. Remove from heat and cool thoroughly. Fold together egg mixture and whipped cream. Pour into soufflé form with a parchment paper collar or aluminum foil rim above the top edge of form. Chill until firm.

Meanwhile, blend raspberries with honey. Strain over unmolded souffle and serve with pride.

Whether or not you can pull this off as a bedside extravaganza is questionable. But it is one uptown, light treat to sample before you put your head on that pillow!

For generations people have gone to sleep with ice cream on the tummy. I know one young man who would understand that statement as a literal fact. He'd take the carton to his bed, get comfy, and eat the ice cream from the carton balanced on his chest.

As a matter of research, I've learned that there are many people who claim ice cream is the winner for a cold treat on a sleepless night.

Carton ice cream may pacify some folks, but discriminating people would much prefer homemade frozen dessert. And there are as many good homemade ice cream recipes as there are families who own freezers.

I've opted to share the recipe that made both my childhood "sleep outs" and church ice cream socials memorable events. Part of the appeal was in the making and the waiting. The rule was that no matter how good it looked, no one was allowed to snitch a sample until the mix turned into ice cream.

Arden Ashton introduced our neighborhood to Mrs. B's Famous Ice Cream. Once it was frozen, you could stay up all night eating that ice cream. To start eating it is to keep eating it until it is gone. Use it as a bedtime snack at your own risk.

Mrs. B's Famous Ice Cream

1 ½ cups lemon juice
2 ½ cups white sugar
1 ½ cups pineapple juice
½ cup crushed pineapple
¹/₈ cup maraschino juice
18 chopped maraschino cherries
½ cups chopped pecans
1 pint canned milk and/or cream

In a large bowl mix lemon juice, sugar, pineapple juice, crushed pineapple, maraschino juice, and maraschino cherries. Allow to stand for an hour until the sugar is dissolved. Pour into six-quart ice cream freezer. Add pecans and canned milk and/or cream. Use milk to fill the rest of the freezer.

Freeze. Eat. Enjoy. Sleep.

I once asked Dr. Ed McKay, who was coming to our house for dinner, what his favorite dessert was.

"Favorite? There is really only one dessert that counts: chocolate eclairs. Chocolate eclairs are like a woman who has charm—if she has it, she doesn't need anything else."

I'm a quick learner. If I served chocolate eclairs the dinner would be a success, whether the rolls flattened, the meat burned, or the salad went limp.

With a recommendation like that for a dessert, I'm certain that eclairs would make any sleepwalker or zombie-eyed, stay-awaker happy at bedtime.

The custard filling can make or break an eclair no matter how much chocolate frosting is swirled across the top. I used my mother's custard recipe for Ed's eclairs. Mother had high standards for custard. According to her, a good custard or a liquid gruel without lumps could cure almost anything.

Maybe that goes for insomnia, too. At least it's worth a try.

There are two parts to this recipe: instructions for making the eclair puff and instructions for the custard filling.

Ed's Eclairs

    1 square butter
    1 cup water
    1 cup flour topped with ¼ tsp salt
    4 eggs

Put butter into boiling water. Stir to melt butter. All at once add flour and salt. Stir vigorously until the mixture is smooth and forms a big, soft ball that holds together. Take pan off the stove for just a few moments to cool custard slightly. Then add eggs, one at a time, beating vigorously after each egg is added. Beat until mixture is smooth.

Grease a cookie sheet. Preheat the oven to 450°. Then drop dough by tablespoon onto the cookie sheet and form into an oblong eclair. Or force dough through pastry bag to make an eclair three-fourths inch wide and three inches long. Bake for fifteen minutes at high heat without opening the oven. Turn heat down to 325° and bake for twenty-five more minutes. Cool on wire rack, fill, and frost with favorite chocolate frosting. Makes eighteen eclairs.

Mother's Custard Filling

⅔ cup sugar
3 slightly beaten eggs
1 tsp flour
2½ cups milk, scalded
¼ tsp salt
2 tsp real vanilla

Combine eggs, sugar, and flour in double boiler. Gradually stir in scalded milk and salt. Cook, stirring constantly, until mixture coats spoon. Remove from heat immediately and add vanilla. Pour into glass bowl and chill well before filling eclairs. This may be made ahead so that it is ready to fill eclairs when they have cooled.

Eclairs seem to digest easily, too, so maybe that is why they are an all-time favorite, the classic bedtime snack—not to be nosed out by a mere chocolate chip cookie. But one of my favorite gentleman friends has another idea.

"Go for the grahams!" counsels Dr. Homer Warner.

Homer is a medical man who is a genius at computer science as a diagnostic help for doctors. He is also an avid athlete, a committed sailor in the Pacific waters, and very fussy about what he eats at bedtime.

He eats only graham crackers.

"I never fuss with the brown box grahams—just the green box," adds Dr. Warner. "It makes all the difference at bedtime."

Consider yourself counseled if you decide to go for the grahams. Graham crackers made with honey have just the right sweetness.

Naturally, the doctor is scientific about how to prepare his bedtime feast.

"Fix 'em and eat 'em!" That's Homer's advice.

Soggy grahams are out. Don't let them soak too long or drown a lone cracker in a big bowl of milk, either. While this snack is about honey-grahams and not milk, Homer emphasizes that to use pale, skimmed stuff and call it milk is to ruin the grahams!

The doctor's method is practiced. No mistakes. No time-consuming busywork. He has *the* mug and *the* spoon, plus the neat stack of crackers still in their sectioned wrapper—ready-to-go. When bedtime comes, he unwinds by following a certain ceremony that has to do with *how* the crackers are put in the container before the milk is poured over.

Dr. Warner insists that a proper presentation of grahams at bedtime is really a lost art. A perfect "fix." It takes practice. One must set his standards high and consider the careful placement of each cracker.

"With the flat side of the spoon one carefully stomps each graham down, so it breaks up just so. No crumbling," cautions Homer, "just nice, orderly breaking-up of the crackers —one cracker at a time as it is settled and stomped on by its neighbor."

My husband has his own demands for bedtime treat. He calls it "Mutsop," which is Postum backwards. He's a "wix your mords" man, and therefore a popular grandfather.

Somehow "Mutsop" is a perfect word for what he likes as a preface to sweet dreams. This is not a hearty, strong-flavored hot drink. "Mutsop" is mild, soothing, and undemanding of one's taste buds and psyche.

Jim has an explanation for people who aren't familiar with his favorite nighttime drink: "You know how it feels when you shake the milk from the baby's bottle onto the inside of your wrist to test the temperature? When it's perfect you don't feel it. Right? Well, that's 'Mutsop.' "

It's the perfect, undemanding, blah-drink!

You begin "Mutsop" by warming the milk and a dash of salt. Then sprinkle Postum across the top gently, lightly, and slowly. The amount used is determined by the color of the drink. Wait between sprinkles for the Postum to dissolve for a true reading of the color! Add sugar the same way, a sprinkle across the top a-little-at-a-time. The test for this is by taste.

If there is any left to pour into a cup, after the taste test, you are fortunate.

Linda Eyre keeps people laughing when she talks about Rick's multiple-meals-a-day. She says she can handle that. What she doesn't cotton to is when he brings one of those meals to bed and eats it there!

It seems to me that Phyllis Diller and Linda Eyre are in the same bed, so to speak. Chomping, like coloring, can jiggle the bed! (See the next chapter, *"Read Me to Sleep."*)

But there you go, gentlemen. Let that be fair warning. Men and women have different ideas on a lot of things. For example, a certain man was in charge of the Scout banquet. When the church banquet tables were all set up and covered with paper and arranged with utensils, salt and pepper shakers, and water glasses, the chairman decided that he had better have his wife come over and check on things, just to be sure it was done right, and that nothing had been forgotten. Starting time was nearly upon him.

She came. As she inspected, she was startled by the bleakness of the setting. No flowers, no decorations. Surely not what a woman would do. She turned to her tired husband and said patiently, "Well, dearie, the tables seem to be set properly, but what are you going to use for a centerpiece?"

At first the man was shaken. He looked at his wife. He looked at his tables. He looked back at his wife. Then he made a swift decision.

"Butter!" he said confidently. "Squares of butter."

Not all men are creative around food. If only desserts and such things can be tackled with success, though life is short—as the billboard on I-15 reminds—it can be sweet.

Especially at bedtime. Sweet dreams.

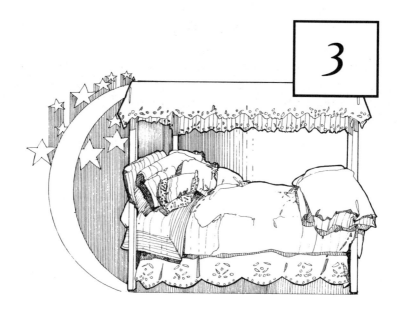

Read Me to Sleep

I once heard a famous talk show host interview Phyllis Diller about her pending divorce from Fang.

"Phyllis," the host said, "I'm sorry about you and Fang. Tell us about this divorce. Whatever happened? Is it anything you can talk about?"

"Oh, I can talk about it all right. It's just that I can't stand people who bring books to bed."

"Fang brings books to bed?"

"Fang brings books to bed."

"But, Phyllis, a lot of people bring books to bed and don't end up in divorce. Reading helps put them to sleep."

Phyllis was sharp in responding to that comment. "Reading I can handle. Coloring pictures jiggles the bed. Fang and I are finished!"

When it is bedtime at your house, though you may not have a Fang in your bed coloring pictures, sleep may still come hard. If so, welcome to the world of very grown-up people.

Reading before sleep may be useful.

But read what?

One day, while working as an editor, the stack of manuscripts loomed large in front of me. The only way to get through such a project is to follow the proverbial "move-the-woodpile" method. You move one log at a time, and one day the job is done.

Doggedly I persisted. Sooner or later, the stack would be flattened.

In that resigned manner, I picked up another short entry to consider publishing in the magazine I was with. It sounded vaguely familiar as I read it through. Strange that it sounded familiar. I looked at the name submitting the piece. Not anyone I'd heard of before, but the work seemed like something I'd read before!

I passed the piece along to someone else in the office and it came back with this note attached: "You galoot! That's your own work. We published it a year ago. Send it back with a letter about plagiarism."

I did just that. But it was a funny feeling to realize that once I write something it is no longer mine—even to me.

As an editor I've learned the value in reading a wide range of work, but certainly not to claim any of it as my own. There are many fascinating things I've read that I like to share, however. Some are included here as appealing reading —the kind you can do in bed before dropping off to sleep.

What I've compiled here are bits and pieces—nothing to keep you awake too long. The excerpts have good morals. A little perspective on self-improvement to mull over through the night can't be all bad.

Especially at bedtime, "The Whistle," by Benjamin Franklin, is thought provoking. Besides everything else that it teaches, it suggests an idea for writing one's life story. The writing is quaint but the concept timeless:

> When I was a child seven years old, my friends on a holiday filled my pocket with coppers. I went directly to a shop where they sold toys for children; and, being charmed with the sound of a *whistle* that I met by the way in the hands of another boy, I voluntarily offered and gave all my money for one. I then came home, and went whistling all over the house, much pleased with my *whistle*, but disturbing all the family. My brothers and sisters and cousins, understanding the bargain I had made, told me I had given four times as much for it as it was worth; put me in mind what good things I might have bought with the rest of the money, and laughed at me so much for my folly, that I cried with vexation; and the reflection gave me more chagrin than the *whistle* gave me pleasure.
>
> This, however, was afterwards of use to me, the impression continuing on my mind, so that often, when I was tempted to buy some unnecessary thing, I said to myself, *Don't give too much for the whistle*: and I saved my money.
>
> As I grew up, went into the world, and observed the actions of men, I thought I met with many, very many, who *gave too much for the whistle*.
>
> When I saw one too ambitious to court favor, sacrificing his time in attendance on levees, his repose, his

liberty, his virtue, and perhaps his friends, to attain it, I have said to myself, *This man gives too much for his whistle*.

When I saw another fond of popularity, constantly employing himself in political bustles, neglecting his own affairs and ruining them by that neglect, *He pays*, indeed, said I, *too much for his whistle*.

If I see one fond of appearance, or fine clothes, fine houses, fine furniture, fine equipages, all above his fortune, for which he contracts debts, and ends his career in a prison, *Alas!* say I, *he has paid dear, very dear, for his whistle*.

In short, I conceive that great part of the miseries of mankind are brought upon them by the false estimates they have made of the value of things, and by their *giving too much for their whistles*.

Reading John Steinbeck can keep you awake. And we wouldn't want to do that! However, the following excerpt from his short story "The Flight" is so well written that it is satisfying reading. Feeling satisfied, you can snuggle up and snooze off until morning.

The story is about Pepe, who is the joy of his widowed mother's life. Although he is only a teenager, already there has been trouble in the village, and Pepe has had to defend himself with his dead father's knife. He comes home, tells his mother the story, and announces:

"I am a man now, Mama. The man said names to me I could not allow."

"Yes, thou art a man, my poor little Pepe. Come! We must get you ready."

Pepe stood silently watching his mother's frantic activity. His chin looked hard, and his sweet mouth was drawn and thin. His little eyes followed Mama about the room almost suspiciously.

Rosy asked softly, "Where goes Pepe?"

Mama's eyes were fierce. "Pepe goes on a journey. Pepe is a man now. He has a man's thing to do."

At last the preparation was finished. The loaded horse stood outside the door. The water bag dripped a line of moisture down the bay's shoulder.

The moonlight was being thinned by the dawn . . . the family stood by the shack. Mama confronted Pepe. "Look, my son! Do not stop until it is dark again. Do not sleep even though you are tired. Take care of the horse in order that he may not stop of weariness. Remember to be careful with the bullets—there are only ten. Do not fill thy stomach with jerky or it will make thee sick. Eat a little jerky and fill thy stomach with grass. When thou comest to the high mountains, if thou seest any of the dark watching men, go not near to them nor try to speak to them. And forget not thy prayers." She put her lean hands on Pepe's shoulders, stood on her toes and kissed him formally on both cheeks, and Pepe kissed her on both cheeks. Then he went to Emilio and Rosy and kissed both of their cheeks.

"Go now," she said. "Do not wait to be caught like a chicken."

Pepe pulled himself into the saddle. "I am a man," he said.

It was the first dawn when he rode up the hill toward the little canyon which let a trail into the mountains. Before Pepe had gone a hundred yards, the outlines of his figure were misty; and long before he entered the canyon, he had become a gray, indefinite shadow.

Mama stood stiffly in front of her doorstep, and on either side of her stood Emilio and Rosy. They cast furtive glances at Mama now and then.

When the gray shape of Pepe melted into the hillside and disappeared, Mama relaxed. She began the high, whining keen of the death wail. "Our beautiful— our brave," she cried. "Our protector, our son is gone" . . . and she turned and went into the house and shut the door.

"We will have no breakfast," said Emilio. "Mama will not want to cook." Rosy did not answer him. "Where is Pepe gone?" he asked.

Rosy looked around at him. She drew her knowledge from the quiet air. "He has gone on a journey. He will never come back."

"Is he dead? Do you think he is dead?"

"He is not dead," Rosy explained. "Not yet."

. . . Gradually the light flowed down over the ridge. . . . Pepe drew up and looked back, but he could see nothing in the darker valley below . . . then . . . without warning Pepe's horse screamed and fell on its side. He was almost down before the rifle crash echoed up from the valley. From a hole behind the struggling shoulder, a stream of bright crimson blood pumped and stopped and pumped and stopped. Pepe lay half-stunned beside the horse. He looked slowly down the hill. Pieces of sage clipped off beside his head and another crash echoed up from side to side of the canyon. . . . Then a white streak cut into the granite of the slit and a bullet whined away and a crash sounded up from below. Pepe felt a sharp pain in his right hand.

Pepe looked into a little dusty cave in the rock and gathered a handful of spider web, and he pressed the mass into the cut, plastering the soft web into the blood. The flow stopped almost at once.

When the sun slid past noon he had not gone a mile. He crawled exhaustedly a last hundred yards to a patch of high sharp manzanita, crawled desperately . . . for safety. His hand was swollen and heavy; a little thread of pain ran up the inside of his arm and settled in a pocket in his armpit. . . . Pepe pulled himself up. The new day was light now. The flame of sun came over the ridge and fell on Pepe where he lay on the ground. His coarse black hair was littered with twigs and bits of spider web. His eyes had retreated back into his head. Between his lips the tip of his black tongue showed.

He lifted his head to listen, for a familiar sound had come to him from the valley he had climbed out of; it was the crying yelp of hounds, excited and feverish, on a trail . . . he arose slowly, swaying to his feet, and stood erect. . . . There came a ripping sound at his feet.

. . . His body jarred back. . . . The second crash sounded from below. Pepe swung forward and toppled from the rock. His body struck and rolled over and over, starting a little avalanche. And when at last he stopped against a bush, the avalanche slid slowly down and covered up his head. (*Short Story Masterpieces* [New York: Dell Publishers, 1954], p. 54.)

It was Rachel Carson who wrote *Silent Spring* and forever after heightened our quality of life by encouraging awareness: ''If I had influence with the good fairy who is supposed to preside over the christening of all children I should ask that her gift to each child be a *sense of wonder* so indestructible that it would last throughout life, an unfailing antidote against the boredom and disenchantment of later years, the sterile preoccupation with things that are artificial, the alienations from the sources of our strength'' (italics added).

Most of us can thank God for sources of strength on earth that hark back to childhood, to experiences with parents. As children we didn't marvel at their strength. Parents were . . . well, parents! They simply were strong! Looking back from our own view as parents, we realize afresh how much we are indebted to our parents for what we are able to do almost automatically.

But that sense of wonder, can you thank parents or a teacher for that? Is it something that can be instilled or is one born with it, like clouds trailing behind from that first world? Where does the love of reading come from in your life? You must have it or you wouldn't be reading now.

Eudora Welty has something to say about reading, something that creates a mood that makes any parent wish for another chance at influencing children through reading. Why, a child who grows up reading turns into a grown-up who knows how to prepare for sleep properly.

The following thoughts are from Eudora Welty's book, *One Writer's Beginnings:*

I learned from the age of two or three that any room in our house, at any time of day, was there to read in, or to be read to. My mother read to me. She'd read to me in the big bedroom in the mornings, when we were in her rocker together, which ticked in rhythm as we rocked, as though we had a cricket accompanying the story. She'd read to me in the dining room on winter afternoons in front of the coal fire, with our cuckoo clock ending the story with "Cuckoo," and at night when I'd got in my own bed. I must have given her no peace. Sometimes she read to me in the kitchen while she sat churning, and the churning sobbed along with *any* story. It was my ambition to have her read to me while *I* churned; once she granted my wish, but she read off my story before I brought her butter. She was an expressive reader. When she was reading "Puss in Boots," for instance, it was impossible not to know that she distrusted *all* cats.

It had been startling and disappointing to me to find out that story books had been written by *people*, that books were not natural wonders, coming up of themselves like grass. Yet regardless of where they came from, I cannot remember a time when I was not in love with them—with the books themselves, cover and binding and the paper they were printed on, their smell and their weight, and with their possession in my arms, captured and carried off to myself. Still illiterate, I was ready for them, committed to all the reading I could give them. (Eudora Welty, *One Writer's Beginnings* [Cambridge, MA: Harvard University Press, 1984], p. 5.)

And now, the perfect bedtime reading, it seems to me, is *To Kill a Mockingbird* by Harper Lee. In fact, I recommend reading the entire book one more time, a little each night, until the entire Pulitzer Prize work has been completed again.

This particular excerpt is about that rare human being. Atticus Finch, who is an attorney in the Deep South during the Depression. It is about his son Jem and his daughter Jean Louise, or Scout, as her father affectionately calls her. And it is about Boo Radley, the unseen, strange, recluse neighbor who leaves homely gifts in a tree knothole for these children one summer.

But it is really about doing unto others—such a good sleepy-time thought. The story is told by Scout, who is eleven years old when this incident takes place.

"Heck? Atticus Finch. Someone's been after my children. Jem's hurt. Between here and the schoolhouse. I can't leave my boy. Run out there for me, please, and see if he's still around. Doubt if you'll find him now, but I'd like to see him if you do. Got to go now. Thanks, Heck."

"Atticus, is Jem dead?"

"No, Scout . . . "

"Jem . . . ?"

Atticus spoke. "He can't hear you, Scout, he's out like a light. . . . "

"Yes sir." I retreated. Jem's room was large and square. . . . The man who brought Jem in was standing in a corner, leaning against the wall. He was some countryman I did not know. He had probably been at the [school] pageant, and was in the vicinity when it happened. He must have heard our screams and come running.

Atticus was standing by Jem's bed.

Mr. Heck Tate [now] stood in the doorway. His hat was in his hand, and a flashlight bulged from his pants pocket. He was in his working clothes.

"Come in, Heck," said Atticus. "Did you find anything? I can't conceive of anyone low-down enough to do a thing like this, but I hope you found him."

. . . Mr. Tate found his neck and rubbed it. "Bob Ewell's lyin' on the ground under that tree down yonder with a kitchen knife stuck up under his ribs. He's dead, Mr. Finch."

"Are you sure?" Atticus said bleakly.

"He's dead all right," said Mr. Tate. "He's good and dead. He won't hurt these children again. . . . Miss Scout, see if you can tell us what happened, while it's still fresh in your mind. You think you can? Did you see him following you?"

". . . all of a sudden somethin' grabbed me an' mashed my costume . . . think I ducked on the ground . . . heard a tusslin' . . . bammin' against the [tree] trunk, sounded like . . . then . . . Mr. Ewell was tryin' to squeeze me to death, I reckon . . . then somebody yanked Mr. Ewell down. . . . That's all I know . . . "

"And then?" Mr. Tate was looking at me sharply.

"Somebody was staggerin' around and pantin' and —coughing fit to die. I thought it was Jem at first, but it didn't sound like him, so I . . . "

"Who was it?"

"Why there he is, Mr. Tate, he can tell you his name."

As I said it, I half pointed to the man in the corner, but brought my arm down quickly lest Atticus reprimand me for pointing. It was impolite to point.

He was still leaning . . . [in the corner] . . . his hands against the wall. They were white hands, sickly white hands that had never seen the sun, so white they stood out garishly against the dull cream wall in the dim light of Jem's room. . . . His cheeks were thin to hollowness; . . . his gray eyes were so colorless I thought he was blind. His hair was dead and thin, almost feathery on top of his head.

. . . When I pointed to him his palms slipped slightly, leaving greasy sweat streaks on the wall. . . . A strange small spasm shook him, as if he heard fingernails scrape slate, but as I gazed at him in wonder the tension slowly drained from his face. His lips parted into a timid smile, and *our neighbor's image blurred with my sudden tears.*

"Hey, Boo" I said.

"Mr. Arthur, Honey," said Atticus, gently correcting me. "Jean Louise, this is Mr. Arthur Radley. I believe he already knows you."

. . . We filed out, first Mr. Tate—Atticus was waiting at the door for him to go ahead of him. . . .

"Come along, Mr. Arthur," I heard myself saying, "you don't know the house real well. I'll just take you to the porch, sir." . . .

I led him through the hall and past the livingroom. "Won't you have a seat, Mr. Arthur? This rocking-chair's nice and comfortable." . . .

I led him to the chair farthest from Atticus and Mr. Tate. It was in deep shadow. Boo would feel more comfortable in the dark.

. . . I sat beside Boo.

. . . Neighbors bring food with death and flowers with sickness and little things in between. Boo was our neighbor. He gave us two soap dolls, a broken watch and chain, a pair of good-luck pennies, and our lives. But neighbors give in return. We never put back into the tree what we took out of it: we had given him nothing, and it made me sad. (Brief excerpt from *To Kill a Mockingbird* by Harper Lee. Copyright © 1960 by Harper Lee. Reprinted by permission of Harper and Row, Publishers, Inc.)

There are lessons to be learned throughout this book: lessons about the influence parents have on their children, their relationships, and the way they show love; lessons about the brotherhood of man, fairness, and more.

I have found both the book and the movie, starring Gregory Peck in the role of Atticus, to be effective teaching tools for my children, and now my grandchildren.

Richard L. Evans once repeated these words of Ralph Waldo Emerson: "I can no more remember all the books I have read than all the meals I have eaten, but they have made me what I am." I heard this when I was a college girl, and I realized how wise it was. I've had a hungry wonder about books all of my life, but this expression put my deep feelings about their worth into descriptive words.

It begins early for the avid reader. A fairy tale with a moral can become part of your moral psyche for the rest of your life. I was six when my parents invested in the volumes of black-bound books — a matched set, each with a color print on the front taken from an illustration inside that particular book. They were *The Book House Books*.

Being the youngest in the family, my sister was the natural heir to the books. Last Christmas, in a fit of Yuletide, she parted with one volume. It was Christmas relived at its height when I opened that package. I was a child again.

The book practically opened by itself to the first page of Hans Christian Andersen's story, *The Emperor's New Clothes*. I had read it so many times in my early days. *Clearly my first emotions surfaced in my heart that Christmas day — I knew then what I know now.* Experience over the years had confirmed my mother's interpretation of the story: the foolishness of vanity; the foolishness of not daring to stand up for what you know is true. Many, many people may know the story but have missed the point altogether. Daily reports in the newspaper prove that. So I include an excerpt of this timely piece because it makes good bedtime reading for adults in these times of scam and scandal:

> Many years ago, there was an Emperor who was so excessively fond of new clothes that he spent all of his money on them.
>
> Life was very gay in the great town where he lived; hosts of strangers came to visit it every day, and among them one day two swindlers. They gave themselves out as weavers, and said that they knew how to weave the most beautiful stuffs imaginable. Not only were the colours and patterns unusually fine, but the clothes that were made of these stuffs had the peculiar quality of becoming invisible to every person who was not fit for the office he held or if he was impossibly dull.
>
> "Those must be splendid clothes," thought the Emperor. "By wearing them I should be able to dis-

cover which men in my kingdom are unfitted for their posts. I shall distinguish the wise men from the fools. Yes, I certainly must order some of that stuff to be woven for me.''

He paid the two swindlers a lot of money in advance so that they might begin their work at once. . . .

The swindlers sat up the whole night before the day on which the procession was to take place, burning sixteen candles, so that people might see how anxious they were to get the Emperor's new clothes ready. They pretended to take the stuff off the loom. They cut it out in the air with a huge pair of scissors, and they stitched away with needles without any thread in them. At last they said: ''Now the Emperor's new clothes are ready!''

''Will your imperial majesty be graciously pleased to take off your clothes,'' said the impostors, ''so that we may put on the new ones, along here before the great mirror.''

The Emperor took off all his clothes, and the impostors pretended to give him one article of dress after the other, of the new ones which they had pretended to make.

Then . . . the Emperor walked along in the procession under the gorgeous canopy, and everybody in the streets and at the windows exclaimed, ''How beautiful the Emperor's new clothes are!''

. . . Nobody would let it appear that he could see nothing, for then he would not be fit for his post, or else he was a fool.

''But he has got nothing on,'' said a little child.

And one person whispered to the other what the child had said. ''He has nothing on. A child says he has nothing on!''

The Emperor writhed, for he knew it was true, but he thought, ''The procession must go on now,'' so he held himself stiffer than ever, and the chamberlains held up the invisible train.

We have just spoken of emperors and of my mother. My mother was Minnie Egan Anderson. Her mother was Evaline Benson Egan. These were two high-principled women in whose lives no foolishness was allowed. But they were fascinated with the lives of others—especially royalty, emperors, queen mothers, and movie stars—who reigned in their own kingdoms of sorts. While Mother and Grandmother passed much judgment back and forth between themselves, still there was incredible compassion for these famous folks "who didn't know any better."

When Wallis Simpson and Edward, earlier Prince of Wales and at the time King of England, were conducting their romance, there had been much media coverage in the United States, much clucking of tongues in many languages that stretched clear to Utah. Even the girls at the University of Utah copied Mrs. Simpson's coiffure—hair parted in the middle with finger waves flat against the head. I tried it one day, feeling very elegant with the outcome, but I must have looked like the original "little head" or worse. Mother wouldn't let me go to grade school that way. Perhaps I was only to feel sorry for sinners and not try to look like them.

This romance between the unmarried English king and the American divorcée came to a head when it became clear that British constitutional/conventional considerations would not permit the king to make this marriage and remain king. The question on every tongue was, "Will he forgo the marriage or will he abdicate?" Each time Grandma came to dinner she and Mother would cluck-cluck some more and hope out loud that duty would be victorious over romance —a point of view heavily imposed upon my young psyche that's had lifelong ripples. "Wickedness never was happiness," they recited to each other. The connection between falling in love and wickedness escaped me at that tender age. The whole thing seemed very romantic to my child's heart.

The day of the radio broadcast to the British people, Grandmother, Mother, and I were gathered around our Majestic to listen in. (Dad was there, too, but he just kept on reading the paper.)

They cried. I did, too, in my own way. Why should duty crowd out love? I was born full of love, but I've since learned much more about life's pain and which one, duty or love, is the winner.

Later Mother took me down to the Paramount Theater to watch the newsreel. And she wept again. Over what? Sin? Mother was dead set against sin! Over lost opportunity? Mother was in favor of snatching opportunity, of taking hold of life at the flow of the tide. Over poor choices? She worked hard at helping people understand their options and the subsequent outcomes so that better choices in life could be made. She taught these at church and in our home to the parade of people coming for help.

Back to Edward and Wallis. There are many poor choices made in the name of love these days. It seems like a great idea to include here a portion of the text of the famous abdication speech to the British people given on December 11, 1936, by Edward VIII:

> At long last I am able to say a few words of my own. I have never wanted to withhold anything, but until now it has not been constitutionally possible for me to speak.
>
> A few hours ago I discharged my last duty as King and Emperor, and now that I have been succeeded by my brother, the Duke of York, my first words must be to declare my allegiance to him. This I do with all my heart.
>
> You all know the reasons which have impelled me to renounce the throne. But I want you to understand that in making up my mind I did not forget the country or the empire, which as Prince of Wales and lately as King, I have for twenty-five years tried to serve.
>
> But you must believe me when I tell you that I have found it impossible to carry the heavy burden of responsibility and to discharge my duties as King as I would wish to do *without the help and support of the woman I love*.

And I want you to know that the decision I have made has been mine and mine alone. This was a thing I had to judge entirely for myself. The other person most nearly concerned has tried up to the last to persuade me to take a different course.

I have made this, the most serious decision of my life, only upon the single thought of what would, in the end, be best for all.

This decision has been made less difficult to me by the sure knowledge that my brother, with his long training in the public affairs of this country and with his fine qualities, will be able to take my place forthwith without interruption or injury to the life and progress of the empire. And he has one matchless blessing, enjoyed by so many of you, and not bestowed on me —a happy home with his wife and children. . . .

I now quit altogether public affairs and I lay down my burden . . . , but I shall always follow the fortunes of the British race and empire with profound interest. . . . And now, we all have a new King. I wish him and you, and his people, happiness and prosperity with all my heart. God bless you all! God save the King! (*An Editor's Treasury*, ed. Herbert R. Mayes, part 1, vol. 2 [New York: Atheneum, 1968], p. 1132; italics added.)

Speaking of empires, we turn now to a memorable picture-piece written by Orville Dewey as part of his work, *Rome's Colosseum by Moonlight*. To anyone who has been to the Colosseum, this catches the flavor. I included it in my personal journal after one of my visits there.

I went to see the Colosseum by moonlight. It is the monarch, the majesty of all ruins; there is nothing like it. All associations of the place, too, give it the most impressive character. When you enter within this stupendous circle of ruinous walls and arches, and grand terraces of masonry, rising one above another, you stand upon the arena of the old gladiatorial combats and Christian martyrdom; and as you lift your eyes to the vast amphitheater, you meet, in imagination, the eyes of a hundred thousand Romans, assembled to witness the bloody spectacles. What a multitude and mighty array of human beings; and how little do we know in modern times of great assemblies! One, two, and three and, at its last enlargement by Constantine, more than three hundred thousand persons could be seated in the Circus Maximus!

. . . What thronging life was here then! What voices, what greetings, what hurrying footsteps upon the staircases of the eighty arches of entrance! And now, as we picked our way carefully through the decayed passes, or cautiously ascended some moldering flight of steps . . . , there was no sound here but of the bat, and none came from without but the roll of a distant carriage, or the convent bell. . . .

It is scarcely possible to describe the effect of moonlight upon this ruin. Through a hundred lonely arches and blackened passageways it streamed in, pure, bright, soft, lambent, and yet distinct and clear, as if it came there at once to reveal, and cheer, and pity the mighty desolation. But if the Colosseum is a mournful and desolate spectacle as seen from within—without, and especially on the side which is the best preservation, it is glorious. We passed around it, and, as we looked upward, the moon shining through its arches, from the opposite side, it appeared as if it were the coronet of the heavens, so vast was it—or like a glorious crown upon the brow of night. (*An Editor's Treasury*, p. 1132.)

Each generation seems to get around to reading something of Durant's histories. A most remarkable experience. At our house we've been reading the volumes straight through for years. Currently with friends, we're studying *Our Oriental Heritage* and finding it incredibly interesting—largely because of the insight and writing style of Will and Ariel Durant. And a special friend gave me a digest volume by the Durants called *The Lessons of History*. It is one of my favorite books, not only because of the giver and the memories it invokes but also because of the wisdom between its covers. For example:

Life is selection. In the competition for food or mates or power some organisms succeed and some fail. In the struggle for existence some individuals are better equipped than others to meet the tests of survival. Since Nature (here meaning total reality and its processes) has not read very carefully the American Declaration of Independence or the French Revolutionary Declaration of the Rights of Man, we are all born unfree and unequal: subject to our physical and psychological heredity, and to the customs and traditions of our group; diversely endowed in health and strength, in mental capacity and qualities of character. (Will and Ariel Durant, *The Lessons of History* [New York: Simon and Schuster, 1968], pp. 19–20. Copyright © 1968 by Will and Ariel Durant; reprinted by permission of Simon and Schuster, Inc.)

Sob! For all with breaking hearts and ironic tests: Beethoven, who goes deaf; the walking man who suffers a stroke; the athlete who falls on the ski slopes and is paralyzed; King Edward, who lived in a time and place when a commoner, a divorcée, was unsuitable to be a companion on the throne!

People have lived on God's earth in many places under varying circumstances, always to battle with nature, with the forces human personalities impose upon each other, with the adversary and his helping angels. Neither centuries and locations nor personalities can alter truth as one finds it in the records of the ancient people of America. Truth is truth wherever it is told, whatever people are the stars of its implementation or its abandonment. Surely there is something for us to be motivated by at bedtime in this reading from 4 Nephi in the Book of Mormon:

The disciples of Jesus had formed a church of Christ in all the lands round about. And as many as did come unto them, and did truly repent of their sins, were baptized in the name of Jesus; and they did also receive the Holy Ghost. . . . And there were no contentions and disputations among them, and every man did deal justly one with another. . . . And there were great and marvelous works wrought by the disciples of Jesus, insomuch that they did heal the sick, and raise the dead, and cause the lame to walk, and the blind to receive their sight, and the deaf to hear; and all manner of miracles did they work among the children of men; and in nothing did they work miracles save it were in the name of Jesus. (4 Nephi 1:1–2, 5.)

There it is! The secret to happiness and peace.

And although it isn't mentioned specifically, it seems to me that a good night's rest would be one of the blessings of such a life-style.

Goodnight, if you can get it!

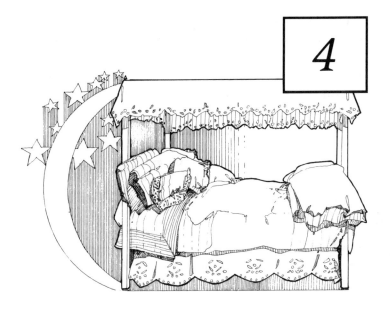

Pipe Dreams

It was summer at a large university. Continuing Education Week was underway, which meant that thousands of adults from all over the world had crowded the campus. The student dormitories had been taken over by the students' parents, young marrieds, family gatherings, singles who hoped to change their status, and women who came in clusters for the lark of it.

I was in a high-rise dorm filled with women on the lark. It was their annual get-away-from-it-all reward. They could eat somebody else's cooking while hubby took the toddlers on at home. They might gain a few pounds, but they'd grow intellectually and spiritually too.

My room was on the ground level in the VIP area since I was one of the lecturers. I had been giving it my all that day, and I was exhausted. Peace . . . quiet . . . sleep . . . that's all I wanted.

It isn't all I got.

In the middle of the night, I was roused by the sound of a bell of some kind. I stirred slightly, decided it couldn't possibly be tolling for me, and rolled onto my other side without opening a lid.

Again I was roused, but this time there was more going on than bells ringing. When I hear clatter, chatter, and commotion at a high pitch, as women laugh and talk, I react. I hate to miss a good time. And besides, they sounded close.

I staggered out of bed and looked out of the window, and suddenly it hit me—that bell was a fire alarm! That's why all those women were standing outside in their nightclothes. I had to get outside, too.

Fire or no fire, when I took the few steps out of my room to the front door, it took maximum self-control to keep from collapsing in laughter. I was facing the most startling scene! The Church women of the world dressed for bed. It was enough to make a person lose his testimony. (Note the gender used.)

Have you ever looked upon hundreds of women surprised from slumber?

There they stood, clutching to their handbags, with their hands folded in front of them. From there on, nothing was the same. Each lady had her own way of keeping covered, comfy, cool, warm, trendy—and anointed. Each had her own special goo smeared on her face. Or if she didn't, the past day's makeup was smeared around instead.

Honestly, they looked like refugees from a survival trek.

There is more. Each woman had a unique way of getting gorgeous for the morrow. I saw everything from hair nets to brush rollers, from rags tied in knots among strands of hair to juice cans clipped into coiffures. There was one with her head swathed in bathroom tissue—it looked as if it were the entire roll.

To be discreet, I won't describe the nighties, the naughties, the quaint and modest gowns, the baby-dolls, the cut-offs, the papa pajamas, the raincoat over underwear. But you name it, it was there.

Thinking about the relationship between those outfits and sleep kept me awake the rest of the night. Good grief, no wonder so many marriages are in trouble!

Mind you, I didn't laugh at all these answers to the pipe dreams of some poor man. How could I? I would have been laughed at right back. But I did change the subject for my lecture the next day.

I called my lecture "Pipe Dreams."

Willa Cather is a favorite author of mine, and she is required reading in certain English classes. Maybe you've read some of her work. She once wrote that there were only two or three human stories and that they go on repeating themselves as fiercely as if they had never happened before.

So do jokes around the dinner table—particularly jokes about marrieds.

I know one happily married couple who tell jokes at bedtime. They laugh themselves to sleep. If it works for them maybe it will work for you, and I will include some in this chapter to get you going.

Meanwhile, this is the way it works: they start off with the old familiars. Then the husband tells her the jokes he heard at work that day. The wife, trained woman that she is, laughs. She learned early on that her marriage depends upon such responses. At least she is no longer required to admit whether she caught on to the story—she just laughs anyway.

Now, that is a happy couple.

Here's a story one woman told in a class at the National Institute of Fitness at the base of the incomparable bulwark, Red Hill, near Santa Clara, Utah.

Did you hear the one about the man who was telling his golf buddy about the strange turn his wife had taken?

"What's happened?" asked the other golfer.

"Oh, she's suddenly become very religious," the husband replied.

"Yeah, how? Chants, finger beads, that kind of thing?"

"No," explained the husband, "but she thinks the bathroom scales are a religious symbol, I guess. Every morning she steps on them and cries out, 'Good Heavens!' "

Marriage itself offers a lot of laughs. Married or not, anyone can get a chuckle—or maybe some sleep—out of this institution and its myths.

Yes, laughing together over shared humor is one way for marrieds to warm up at bedtime. Some couples deliberately rehearse the day's happenings to find the humor in them. It can be a great marriage-saver as well as a sleep-inducer, learning to laugh together at yourselves.

My sister, Nadine, tells about the time years ago when wigs for women were the big trend. Her son Richard was a toddler, and she'd just finished dressing him for church and had turned her attention to preparing herself. She put her wig on the bed while she slipped into her sweater. Blinded by the pullover, she didn't see Richard drag the wig to the bathroom and drop it in the toilet.

It was bedtime before Nadine could tell her husband why they were so late for church, and Cal awakened the children with his guffaws.

Jessie Evans Smith told me about the following exchange with her husband that kept them laughing together at bedtime for years. It's worked at our home, too.

Jessie said that she and her husband, Joseph Fielding Smith, were sitting quietly one day in the late evening of their lives. "I was bored," explained Jessie. So she turned to Joseph Fielding, who was studying the scriptures, and said: "Come on, Joseph, take me to the zoo."

"Jessie," he responded, "when they want you, they will come for you."

On the other hand, Eleanor Roosevelt said something that I have used a thousand times in classes for people looking for new life in the marriage relationship. I learned about it on a visit to Valkyr, Mrs. Roosevelt's private retreat at Hyde Park, New York. She said that to be the butt of humor from the other spouse doesn't need to hurt if you've learned to laugh at yourself. "Nobody can make you feel inferior without your consent," said Mrs. Roosevelt.

I remember the first time in public my husband called me by his favorite name for me: Bearcat. There was shocked laughter among some in the room. Then one asked him why that particular name for such a harmless, pregnant old gal.

My Jim explained, "I once saw a Stutz-Bearcat in the antique auto museum in Detroit. I loved it! My wife has a spare tire these days, too, so I call her Bearcat."

For years that gag has brought us a lot of laugh mileage.

My father was a great storyteller and always had a quick line to soften a tense situation. I well remember when my mother was first learning to drive. It was very exciting for all of us. One day Dad came home from work to learn that Mother had crunched a fender and curled the running board on the garage door as she'd tried to back out.

At the table he said: "Well, children, your mother's had herself a day. Tangling with a garage door can injure your pride. But that's nothing to what happened yesterday in traffic. She stalled the car and a policeman came over to scold her into moving along because she was hindering the flow of traffic.

" 'I can't,' cried Mother. 'I don't remember what to do.' [Mother was never very calm under pressure.]

" 'Well, use your noodle, lady! Use your noodle.'

" 'Where is it? Where is it? I've tried every gadget I can find.' "

Dad's favorite joke—or so it seemed because he told it every chance he got, over and over and over until his death—was about the man who walked along the street, looking downcast. An old school chum stopped him and said, "Say, aren't you Tom Brown?"

"Yes."

"I'm glad to see you, but whatever is making you look so miserable and downhearted?"

The dejected man explained that his wife had just died, and that she was his third one to die.

"You have had three wives die? How dreadful. How did they die?"

"The first two died from eating poisonous mushrooms."

"My goodness. And this last one—how did she die?"

"Well, it was a bump on the head."

"It must have been *some bump*!" exclaimed the friend. "How did it happen?"

"Well, she wouldn't eat her mushrooms."

So, it's an old joke. Roll over and go to sleep.

It was a college reunion. It was too many years ago to print, but the topics of conversation had changed over the years from who was killed in the war and who had the newest baby to who was still alive when they didn't show up for the gathering!

"My whole life has passed in review this weekend," lamented one long-since coed.

"You look familiar. Do I know you?" asked a former hotdog skier and fraternity boy.

"You ought to. I wore your pin for six months," the grown-up and grown-older girl replied. She attributed his forgetfulness to early senility or Alzheimer's.

One of the class comics doing the honors as emcee related this personal story:

As his family sat at breakfast, a daughter was talking about her date the night before. She had been taken to a great, new restaurant. The father asked her where it was—he thought that if it was such a good place he ought to take her mother there for a fine meal.

"I really can't tell you, Dad. It's out south of town somewhere. I was enjoying the ride, the scenery, and the company, and all of a sudden we were there."

"I understood perfectly," continued the emcee/father. "That's exactly how her mother and I arrived at just past middle age!"

Traveling *without* my husband while fulfilling professional and church assignments has put me in the company of many kind and gracious married couples who act as hosts. Being the "extra" woman on such occasions, I can be objective about the interaction between husband and wife. No doubt about it: couples develop their own game plans, which isn't to say that they're always pleasant. But to an outsider looking in, much of what goes on is laughable—or would be, if it didn't border on dead serious.

More than one couple endure the problem of the wife answering for the husband—answering and interrupting. It doesn't matter whether it concerns *his* church assignment, *his* business or profession, or *his* anything else, Mrs. Charming has the answers. Even when questions are addressed specifically to him, she's the first to the mike.

This problem seems to be a common one. On one occasion in a social gathering of husbands and wives, I was complaining about such women. One man came up with a solution—divorce and destruction not being options, of course:

"The next time a wife answers for her husband to the point of annoyance, somebody ought to say to her: 'Honey, next time just put your hand behind his neck to work his jaw. But don't let your lips move so much. It makes for a better ventriloquist act!' "

We all laughed and hoped for the best. The man confessed that he and his wife got the idea from an old collection of jokes that they were reading before bedtime.

"What do the simple folk do" at bedtime when sleep simply won't come? Well, they share stories and laugh together.

One of my favorite stories is the one about two wholesale grocers who were talking about the bedtime problems one of them was having.

"Buy her some lingerie as a surprise gift. It works miracles," the counseling friend promised.

Later he asked his friend how things were going at home. "Your suggestion of lingerie for my wife wasn't so good," the man replied.

"Oh? What didn't she like?"

"Well, I don't know if it was the red flannel or the long legs. She never said. She just took them back in a huff."

A winter ago, I was in Palm Springs, California, and the natives carefully explained an interesting traffic problem. I was being driven home from a meeting in a white Fleetwood, and the driver was intent on the news he was sharing because the traffic was clogging up the entire main street.

"There are so many Cadillacs and Lincoln Continentals being driven by old-timers who have retired here that the accident statistics are enormous," said my friend. "Insurance companies are way behind in their claims because there are so many," he added.

We laughed when he admitted that he was one of them.

Then he told me the favorite story circulating in Palm Springs. It seems that a man let his visiting mother-in-law borrow his steel-gray Lincoln—how else could he keep his wife by his side in the evening? As far as he was concerned, his mother-in-law had long since worn out her welcome, and letting her take the car for a day was one way to get her out of the house.

But that car was the pride of his heart and it was intended to be the last car of his life, the investment that would be his until he died, or quit driving.

Anyway, she took the car. Soon after, the word came to him that his mother-in-law had rolled the car off the mountain pass to Hemet. The car was totaled and she was killed.

At least that's the way he told the story—not the other way around, as in "mother-in-law killed and car totaled." First things first.

"I didn't know how to feel," the man said, "Sad or glad. I had mixed emotions."

Foley Richards has won a reputation for being the best clean-joke teller, the man with the best timing when telling a story in his social and business circles. He's committed to the idea that a good joke at bedtime does wonders for setting the thermostat for a peaceful night's sleep and a happier tomorrow.

He told this one one night at a dinner party just after the waiter had taken the orders. The joke takes place in a hotel dining room where a waiter is taking orders from a glum, conversationless couple—obviously married:

"What will you have, sir?"

"Roast beef."

"Baked potato or rice?"

"Baked potato."

"Sour cream, butter, or the works?"

"The works."

"Soup or salad?"

"Soup."

"And what about the vegetable?"

Without batting an eyelid, the husband replied, "Oh, she'll have the same."

I let my daughter talk me into going on the new Star Wars ride at Disneyland. We stood in line for an hour to get in and then hung on to each other for dear life once the eventful ride got under way. It seemed so realistic as we zoomed out over city skyscrapers and whooshed on into space. Incredible!

All the time I kept thinking about a hilarious story that really describes the basic difference between men and women. It's so true to life that it is, indeed, laughable. Try it on your spouse tonight and see if it doesn't improve your bedtime moods.

A husband and wife went to a 3-D film presentation in a science exhibit at a World Exposition. It was a spectacular experience with sight and sound and reality. A thrilling roller coaster ride opened the film. The audience felt as if they were on that coaster themselves. All the sensations of climbs, curves, speed, and downhill slams had the wife reeling in minutes. She put her hand over her mouth and muttered to her husband, "I've got to get out of here."

"Sit down, silly," said the annoyed husband. "It's only a movie!"

Once again the roller coaster roared down a steep incline and careened around a sharp curve. Up the wife stood again.

"Sit down! Sit down! I told you it's just a movie."

"I can't take any more. Let me out."

He pushed her back into her seat and a moment later the film followed the climb of the coaster to precarious new heights before it nearly flew down the other side of the braced track. "Let me out!" she whimpered. "This is me leaving." And she nudged over his legs.

"Listen," the husband whispered angrily, "you sit down and sit still before we both fall out of this thing and get killed!"

At church one Sunday the bishop announced the schedule of events for the holiday season, including a rousing promise that the Christmas party was going to be just for grown-ups that year. Dancing would follow dinner and it would be strictly a dress-up affair.

One wag put his arm around his wife and snuggled her to him, "Honey, would you like to go to that dance?" (I happen to know this man well.)

Now, dancing was her favorite thing and she hadn't been to a dance for years. She was overcome with joy at this question but roused herself to reply, "Would I? I'll say I would!"

And he squeezed her shoulders, laughing, "Well, then, I hope somebody asks you to go!"

My husband never got over his high-school style.

Sitting at the airlines gate waiting for departure can be boring business unless you are into people watching, like I am. On one trip I noticed a handsome, middle-aged couple walk into the area. Obviously the man had been financially successful; both he and his wife were elegantly dressed. But it was just as obvious that he didn't run his home as he ran his business. She led the way into the waiting area and she chose the seats—again and again.

He was meek and attentive. She chose a seat across the room, and he followed behind her like a Red Cross St. Bernard with a medic bag on his neck. Only he had her cosmetic case in one hand and her umbrella and Bloomingdale's shopping bag in the other. Mere minutes passed and she got up and moved to another seat. Her mister padded right behind. Each time she found a place, there was a draft or no ash tray or the sun streamed into her eyes—whatever. She'd sit a minute and then get up and move to another place. Wherever she went, her lamb of a husband was sure to go.

Then, she got up again and this time moved toward the exit gate. He dared to speak, "Where are you going now?"

"I'm going to the newsstand to buy you a book. You've almost finished reading the one you have now."

And that grown-up, that man of means and power in some circles, raised his chin to look into her eyes and asked meekly, "I have?"

And believe me, the people in the waiting area laughed together. The lady must have thought she was his mother. Nanny? Nursemaid? Queen bee? Well, if she tucks him in with a glass of warm milk when bedtime comes . . . say, that may not be all bad!

Insurance friends of mine tell the following story to new customers. It's an old shoe, as stories go, but it has a good moral for grown-ups. Wives really should know more about their husband's financial arrangements during these days of complicated tax structure. Yet not many seem to, and that is what makes the joke so funny.

When an insurance rep moved into a new neighborhood, he began calling on all the couples over fifty to check their portfolios. At one home the husband was away, but the wife invited the salesman/neighbor in. They visited for a moment and then he said, "Do you know the present value of your husband's insurance package? This is my specialty and I'd like to be a good neighbor and help you, if you feel you need it."

"I don't even know what you mean," the confused woman said.

"That's the point. For example, what if your husband should pass away . . . what would you get?"

The little lady thought a moment and then said brightly, "Oh! I know. I'd get a poodle."

Heaven will come soon enough for all of us, which reminds me of the wonderful story LaMont Richards told me about his father, Elder LeGrand Richards of the Council of the Twelve. Elder Richards had been ailing and his life's perspective was beginning to focus on the time of transition between earth and heaven.

One evening, from his sick bed, he wondered aloud to watchers by his bedside: "What if I get to heaven and it is so crowded I can't find my sweetheart, Inie? What'll I do?"

"If Elder Richards, who understands the system the way he does, hasn't figured out the whole thing yet, what chance is there for the rest of us?" asked a friend.

Speaking of dying and going to heaven, something happened at the Pioneer Memorial Theater one evening that had a certain lady talking in those terms.

A woman was sitting in her place waiting for the curtain to go up, when suddenly she felt the wig she was wearing being lifted from her head. She reached to retrieve her portable beauty aid, turning in her seat to see who the tease was.

There was no tease. It was a General Authority and his wife slipping politely by those already in place to their own seats in the center of the row. As they passed behind this certain lady, her wig got caught on the button of the man's coat.

The wig moved along with them! It wasn't until he sat down that he realized what had happened.

People laughed. The lady gasped and with her hands tried to cover her hair, which was bobby pinned flat against her head to accommodate the wig.

One woman was overheard to say: "If that had happened to me and that man's suit button had caught in *my* hair, I'd be so excited I'd have died and gone to heaven!"

Some pipe dream! Wigs are making a comeback though. Maybe she'll have her chance yet.

Meanwhile, sleep well.

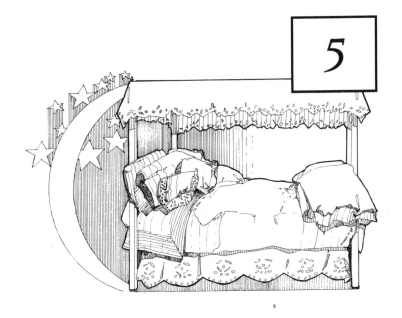

I'll See You in My Dreams

Leonard Bernstein once described his acute interest in people as being so compelling that seeing a person climbing the side of a mountain could make the whole mountain disappear for him.

Rudyard Kipling had something to say on most subjects, and "people" was no exception. He had reverent feelings about mankind which he translated into poetry. His following lines have been paraphrased many times:

For as we come and as we go
(and deadly soon go we!)
The people, Lord, *Thy* people,
Are good enough for me!

I've met some fabulous people: some royalty and some more royal by nature than even birthright allows. Some are famous. Katherine Hepburn *is* radiant in real life, too. Nancy and Ronald Reagan *are* charming. Robert Redford *is* as handsome as he looks on screen. And cooperative, too. My daughters are tall, and when he agreed to pose with them before my camera, he stood on the top step and they stood on the step two down.

Some of the people I've met are local, some are from exotic countries, but it's the people that make the difference.

I'm sure you can say that too. Wherever we grew up, wherever we have lived, worked, traveled, gone to school, served in the military, preached, performed, or established a life, certain people stand out when we think about a time and a place.

Down the hill and across the world are people who have marked my life well, and so I see them in my dreams. Maybe my memories, my adventures, will trigger some of your own. Remembering is such a pleasant sleeping capsule.

Down the hill from the home of my childhood there lived a family who were hard hit by the financial crash of 1929. They were unlikely candidates for the wrenching of such an event since they were small-town people who scarcely had heard of stocks and bonds, much less owned any. But wrenched they were, caught in the wake of bank crashes and a depressed economy.

They had moved to Salt Lake so that the father could start a bricklaying business. For a time, all went well. The big house and the happy family were signs of his success. But then his business collapsed. They introduced the Depression to our neighborhood. And we all watched carefully, in sympathy, with curiosity, and under personal threat.

As the years passed they finally lost everything but each other, as the saying goes. In some families the "each other" part slips away as well, under the weight of hardship.

This family seemed to handle their depressed days well. Maybe that's one reason I remember them so clearly.

The day the living room plush sofa and armchair set and the Oriental rugs were carried away by the furniture store's company truck, I was there taking it all in. I was curled up on a wide brick wall that closed in the front steps and supported the balcony of the second story. It was amazing to note that tears rolled down the face of the father instead of the lady of the house. She bit her lip and narrowed her eyes—that was all. However, the next day she put a henna pack on her baby-soft hair.

The red hair turned her into something I hadn't thought she was, and I never got used to it. Nor did the man. At first he laughingly jabbed at her about it. Then I noticed he'd look at her and shake his head. Then he seemed to let it go, maybe as an act of bravado. At least and at last, that is how I choose to remember it.

The red hair and the daily dusting and polishing of the hardwood floors in the living and dining rooms were the brave gestures against deprivation. The hair was something less beautiful to my eyes, but those floors were impressive.

The only way into the rest of the house was through one end of the living room, where a little entrance hall was formed from the front door to the kitchen door and framed the railing of the stairs to the bedrooms. And there was a walk-in coat closet.

The furniture that was left in the living room included the Majestic radio, and a sturdy, tall-backed, oak rocker faced away from the shiny oak arches that separated the two front rooms. The living room flowed through these arches into the generous dining room that was windowed all around. We could see the Great Salt Lake on the horizon and the railroad tracks just a mile or two below the hill where we all lived. We noticed the view more with the rooms empty.

And we noticed those shiny hardwood floors. What an impact this had on me! So deeply did this situation affect my dream time that in every home my husband and I have lived in, polished hardwood floors have been an important feature.

There were other things this family had to live with, besides the gleaming floors, of course. They had each other. There was a girl, who was my friend, and four or five husky boys who could swallow a quart of milk straight from the bottle in the Frigidaire. At one sitting they could make a super-sized yellow cake disappear, washing it down with whatever homemade root beer they could get their hands on. (The mother hid it all over the house.)

About that yellow cake . . .

Sometimes the grocer would let the mother have eggs and chocolate, and she'd bake one of her famous cakes. She'd make one for the grocer, too, because that's how she got the chocolate. He was a widower and would get a hankering for something sweet. She didn't have money to buy luxuries like chocolate, so it was a good deal, and in the process I learned how to make yellow cake and real fudge frosting from scratch and by hand. That means without an electric mixer!

The day the cake was made was always a happy one. A drizzle of batter or frosting on a child's finger is a lovely treat.

The kitchen had furniture. The round oak extension table had been their grandmother's, so it wasn't taken away. There were assorted chairs that the boys straddled backwards at the table. We played Pit. They glued their balsawood model airplanes. We all shelled peas, and snapped beans from the garden, and cracked dried apricot pits to use as nuts in cookies. And one of the boys wrote endless, sticky rhymes on brown wrapping paper torn into sheets of sorts. They were sent farther down the hill to the blonde girl, fragile, frail, and romantic. And nobody teased or tortured him about it.

You see, love was a part of their life-style. Everybody made everybody feel good.

Like the Jewel Tea Company man who'd come to call. He'd prolong his visits there, it seemed to me, talking and laughing at great length, though the mother scarcely bought a bottle of vanilla from him. But he'd leave her plenty of samples before shortcutting beneath the big Potawatomi plum tree as he left. Sometimes the father walked with him a way with an arm around his shoulder.

In the end, this family seemed better off than most in the neighborhood. Though they were slammed the hardest by financial disaster, they were shining examples because of their love.

The father and mother really loved each other. Next to my parents, they are my earliest recollection of a couple in love, outside of the movies.

I told you about the rocker that was left by the radio in the living room. The man would sit there a lot—though he wasn't an old man—rocking, rocking. Sometimes I'd see the woman sitting on his lap, and they'd be laughing and "loving each other up" as they called it. On such a day I never noticed the emptiness.

When trouble comes, everyone should have a kind of rocker in which to stack up and love away the hurt.

Mulling over scenes and people from one's childhood works as comfort for the insomniac. Try travel memories too. It's worth staying awake awhile just to have time to recall what guides for life you have picked up along the road.

I've learned valuable things in Israel, and the only time sufficient to dwell upon them is last thing at night. Walking where Jesus walked, following the route where the cross was carried, strolling beside the Sea of Galilee, and pondering miracles both of the Savior's day and in one's own life. Studying the generations of stones in walls and buildings, where beauty comes not in the uniforming of material from foundation to roof but in the thrifty use of ancient stones mixed with contemporary materials. There history unfolds at a glance — thousands of years of man on the earth.

Figuratively speaking, walking in the footsteps of Christ is trying to be like him. Literally walking where Jesus walked brings forth tender feelings of understanding, gratitude, and certitude that he lived. Those same stones were beneath *his* feet, too, and they are now trampled by natives who have long since forgotten that this ground is sacred. And sacred it is to a pilgrim like me.

Sometimes there will be a tour guide whose profession keeps his heart remembering. Being with starry-eyed tourists in Jerusalem is different from being a tour guide anywhere else. The visitors bring a special spirit with them.

On one of my trips to the Holy Land our group had an Arab guide whose family was among the first group ever to be converted to Christianity in the Holy Land. And he was a chain-smoker.

At first he was very angry that we wouldn't allow him to smoke around us. He debated whether to take the assignment, but we discussed it and were able to work out a suitable arrangement for all. By the end of the second day of constant companionship with our guide, he noticed that we got along fine without cigarettes. He noticed that he was a slave to his. And he enjoyed being with us. We were "different" and he wanted to know why. By the fourth day we were talking freely about how he could quit smoking. We were his welcome conscience. We planned different surprises as substitutes for cigarettes, and busy work for empty hands: a US ballpoint souvenir, a letter opener, red licorice brought from home in someone's suitcase.

By the end of the two weeks he didn't smoke at all during the time he was with us — not even to sneak off to the side for a smoke while we shopped.

"What will I do when you have gone?" he cried.

He explained to me that after we left he'd be with another group who wouldn't care about him as we had—who would, in fact, encourage him to smoke because they did.

"Make your own rules and announce them at the beginning," I encouraged. "Why should the Holy Land be littered with the cigarette butts of the nations of the world?" He agreed. So then we loaded him up with spiritual support—tracts, books, and cassette-taped memories of our prayers, songs, and personal testimonies.

I see this guide in my dreams because he represents a vast population down the hill and across the world who have never been taught such lifesaving techniques and, like him, would welcome such understanding.

Across the world I have walked where noble women have struggled and substituted to make homes for their families. To learn how to help them better, I have visited them in their homes—humble, grand, convalescent, institutional, communal, shared, and lonely. Cooking at their stove brings understanding.

In the deep inland of the People's Republic of China, the hearth is still the center of the home. It is the source of power, warmth, hospitality, and what small comfort is theirs.

In a commune that produced tea, the homes of the peasants were not only stark but also centuries old in style and convenience. But they proudly showed my group the efficiency of their hearths. It reminded me of an outdoor barbecue that people built in their backyards during the fifties when the war was sufficiently behind everyone and having fun was in fashion again.

One stove we saw in China had a raised firebox so that the woman didn't have to stoop to add fuel. *That* was her proud convenience—that and her stooped husband who brought her dried sticks, which the worn peasant woman would toss into the lively fire.

It was a show-off fire for us tourists, I am sure. But my interpreter assured me that the fire was kept going all the time because it was inefficient not to keep a light. Besides, it gave the venerable man of the house something to do. Women worked the fields, worked in the tea factory, and worked at the stove.

So back and forth he shuffled, in and out of the hearth area, with a single bundle of twigs and reeds each time. It seemed inefficient, yet it allowed frequent eye contact between the two. Each time he returned and handed the fuel to her, their eyes met. The looks they exchanged spoke of the years of unfailing care for each other, body and soul. It was an act of intimacy, of sacred giving in their respective roles to meet each other's needs.

It was like being stirred all over again by Louise Rainer's Academy Award performance in Pearl Buck's *The Good Earth*. Unforgettable, unspoken emotion.

Yes, I see the Chinese couple in my dreams, especially on the nights when I am evaluating my own role as a woman and my husband's role as man of the house in a world that encourages impersonal independence.

Sometimes when I can't sleep, I think of great women across the world who spend their lives working outside their homes (in addition to within their homes) to raise the standard of living for their sisters.

Like Grace, for example.

I can see Grace now. She was deep black and had snapping eyes alive to life. She was an African who took a Christian first name when she entered government service and began representing her nation at international meetings.

Women from seventy-four countries of the free world gathered in Kiel, Germany, for the International Council of Women Conference. The agenda was full. Emotions ran high because there was a certain dichotomy. Life in emerging countries can't compare to the industrialized world. At first, understanding was hard to come by. Each time the council met, it was in a different place in the world. At each conference, there were many first-time delegates and the bond of trust had to be established all over again. Although this slowed progress, it allowed education for a broader spectrum of women.

Those of us who were "old-timers" watched the process with interest as we tried to move things along.

For example, I remember the dramatic moment when an experienced delegate from Canada reported on the fervor of North American women for the cause of equality.

"Why," said she with quivering lips, "there even have been bonfires upon which some women have tossed their unique undies, symbolic of their need to be treated with the same considerations as men—same rights, same salaries, same privileges under the law, in education and work force benefits."

There was an outbreak of applause.

Then, Grace stood up, commanding attention from the group. She was tall, regal, smiling. She was in her native costume, which was swathed about her head and body in brightly patterned batik. She spoke softly in flawless English with a British accent. She curried empathy. (Americans who travel are startled to learn that British English is what people speak from Scandinavia to Africa—our own dialect is . . . our own.)

Grace spoke: "To seek equality with men is a long walk down the path for us. To garner the vote for women will come in another day. What our women need is water—pure water for their families. We need water closer than a two-mile walk from home. We need answers to the impelling question of high infant mortality. How *can* we keep our babies alive longer? What can we do about high infant mortality and short-lived adults?"

The convention body was still.

Suddenly everything was in perspective. Keeping babies alive is top priority, but there quickly follows the question of what comes next. Alive for what? How can we help people to feel loved through growing up, loved through marriage and mating, loved and secure through the dwindling of life's last days?

Ilse of Germany had some ideas. She spoke about the truth in the traditional understanding of Christian nations that all people on the earth are God's children. And we should be more worried about the well-being of the spirit of mankind in the world than equality in a small corner of it.

Ilse was a university professor who didn't look the part as we've come to know it. She lived alone, which was exactly what she wanted, and it showed. She dressed only to please herself in comfortable, beautifully-made, coarse hand-knits in vague colors. Her one garment was styled like a Polynesian muumuu capable of hiding a multitude of lumps. A matching scarf was knit sufficiently long to twist high about her neck and drape fore and aft with thick fringe trim. It was her sole protection against dropping temperatures.

"Who knows of the layers I have underneath?" was her jovial reply when I asked her if she didn't need a coat. Her heart was layers of warmth too.

Have you ever been to Ephesus? I wish everyone could see Ephesus and feel the insignificance of the work of man in God's world, seeing proof across the centuries of the fate of civilizations.

Ephesus, that inimitable marble city: marble streets, marble gymnasiums, marble libraries, marble halls of fame and seats of government, marble public baths and toilets, marble brothels, marble marketplaces, marble theaters, marble statues and benches. And the marble amphitheater that will still seat as many people as the Marriott Center at Brigham Young University. Its acoustics are as clear as the Salt Lake Tabernacle's, and there is no longer a roof to cap the sound.

This is the very place, that historic theater, where Paul taught of Christ while the furor against him grew. The industrialists of that day, protecting their thriving industry of icons of Diana, "all with one voice about the space of two hours cried out, 'Great is Diana of the Ephesians.' "

I often think of Ephesus and of the courage of our guide, Akar.

He was a Turk according to my storybook images conjured up from childhood tales of lamps, intrigue, incredible riches, lapis blue turrets, and golden towers. He had the sharp, raw profile, strong jaw, and bald head that illustrators of fairy tales and exotic stories used. But he was nattily dressed in western clothing. Dare I suggest he was a reasonable facsimile of Telly Savalas?

Our group sat in the amphitheater for a little worship service in a place as old as the sacrament itself. I was a watchperson on the tower, the tourist assigned to keep tabs on the guides while the sacrament was being prepared, lest they become bored by the delay and leave us. The Turks were new at limited travel trade, comparatively speaking, so we were at their mercy. Several bus loads of people at prayer and sacrament, with eyes closed and hearts tuned to God, could be left stranded.

Akar, as we called him, sat apart from the boisterous guides and drivers who were rising to the occasion of mockery. Loud laughter, jeers, jokes in a foreign language, left no doubt as to the object of spurn. In our naiveté, we had hoped to move these men by our devotion. Instead they were kin, indeed, to the silversmiths of Ephesus who gathered in this same amphitheater to ridicule Paul.

Fantastic acoustics are a disadvantage under such circumstances. Not only could they hear the sacrament prayer in their places at the top of the amphitheater, but also the sound of their sneering carried down to the level of the table and its officiators. I moved closer to the group and asked them in a level voice to keep their conversations to a whisper. They laughed raucously in response.

It was at this point that Akar arose and walked over to the others, speaking in a tone and manner that even I could understand, though the language was lost to me.

They left the theater, but our guide stayed.

After the meeting I thanked him. He was mellow in answering.

"I haven't been taught to understand the things that you do, but I felt something wholesome here."

"Then I have a gift for you," I said. I had been thinking what I could do to let him know of our gratitude—and of Christian truth. I shyly handed him my pocket-sized New Testament. He handled it reverently and nodded his delight. He watched me write a brief testimony and message addressed to him. I told him how valuable it was to me and how I hoped it would come to be important in his life also.

For the rest of the trip he would pat the pocket of his jacket, which held the New Testament, and he'd smile his appreciation for the gift. Who knows what will become of the book and the Turk who had the courage to position himself against the countrymen in defense of the Christians.

Some nights when sleep doesn't come, turning our thoughts away from self to the plight of others stirs feelings of personal gratitude. What better way to doze off than thanking Heavenly Father for all we have?

Love and loyalty, survival and struggle take different roads in different cultures. In Bangkok I saw children who had been crippled deliberately to evoke pity. They had been trained to beg. They were pushed along the ground toward a likely handout. Dirty little hands outstretched above grotesquely twisted legs could be good business with naive tourists.

"The better to eat with, child!" I could almost hear the parent command as the child was pushed out from a shop door toward our group. How could I ever forget the pleading dark eyes of child after child on the crosswalk bridge and the streets? We were being shown this exotic city by a young friend who was working with the Pearl Buck Foundation to assist children who had been fathered and apparently abandoned by U.S. servicemen, long since sent back to America. Mike told startling stories about what people do in the name of love. His work was to try to lessen the inevitable pain of separation. His reward was to see the joy of reunions and the satisfaction among people who generously contributed to the cause. Mike had a smile that helped him to win battles and to soften hearts, which was probably more of a challenge. Listening to him talk put me in the role of student, though I had been his den mother just short years before.

We visited a silk shop, which was almost overwhelming to me because of its contrast to the scenes of the streets; and also because I used to own a fabric store and I love natural fibers in the same way some people admire figurines. Such beauty! The colors, the weaves, the sheen, the wide variety of elegance from the spinning of a silk worm, enhanced by the artistry of mankind.

I fingered the heavy upholstery-weight silks; the nubby raw silks; the fragile, sheer dress-weight bolts; the exquisite florals; and the novelty weaves. And then I saw my treasure. It was a pillow cover in gray and white silk, subtle and lovely. Embroidered in flowing script were these words of Brahma:

"When the one man loves the one woman and the one woman loves the one man, the very angels leave heaven and come and sit in that house and sing for joy."

When sleep doesn't come, wide-awake dreaming can produce valuable reminders of precious principles of the gospel.

There was a sight in Taiwan that gave me a dramatic perspective towards agency and accountability.

I was in a village hotel several floors up, leaning out of the window to watch a steady parade of the beautiful children of Taiwan on their way to school. From my vantage point I could see the school some distance away. The children knew the school was there, though they couldn't see it yet, and, of course, they were unaware of my presence.

These dark-haired children were charming in the official school uniform: short navy skirt or pants; clean, starched, white shirt; and on this rainy day, a canary-yellow slicker. Some of the children carelessly dragged their slickers behind them; a few let them fly open; others wore them tightly buttoned, like the whole armor of God.

The path the children were taking through the rice paddy was well trampled, but there were big mud puddles and exciting places to hide between tall rushes.

In a variety of sizes, the youthful army came around the corner of the hotel—wave after wave of these little people of Heavenly Father's family who lived in Taiwan. *According to their agency,* they dawdled along, were detoured by the slightest distraction, or else pressed toward the mark—the school way up ahead. It was up to them now; parents weren't around.

To watch the children deal with their environment was to see a slice of life in any age group, in any country, at any given time in the history of man.

Some of the children deliberately plowed right through the deep mud puddles time and again, and came forth filthy.

Others automatically marched around the puddles, almost oblivious to them.

Many absolutely could not resist the temptation to gingerly touch a toe in the mire. One little girl, afterwards, stooped over and tried to wipe the mud from her shoe, then from her hand; then she brushed the spot on her clothes where she had wiped her hand. *Mud is tough to erase.*

Life from a window. Agency and accountability. They made their choices, and so do we.

We are like children walking a path in the rain. We can walk in or around the mud of life as we desire, but with our choices come the consequences. And we are rapidly becoming what we are choosing to be for all eternity.

Spiritual maturity is understanding that we cannot blame anybody else for our actions.

It was the International Year of Women Conference in Houston, Texas. The Utah delegation, of which I was part, was seated in the front, left side, facing the podium in the enormous convention center. Here were the women from America, elected by their neighbors at state conventions to consider issues important to women.

Whatever else this event turned out to be — a government-funded fiasco for women to have a public tantrum or an impassioned effort at consciousness raising — it was an education for me.

From our vantage point down front we could see and hear much that was missed by others. It was a stacked conference. The celebrities of the event were interviewed by the press in the aisle next to our seats: Bella Abzug, Rep. Barbara Jackson, Gloria Steinem, Betty Friedan, Archie Bunker's "Edith" (Jean Stapleton), Martin Luther King's Coretta — who hugged us after we took a stand in favor of black women. Rosalyn Carter, Betty Ford, and Lady Bird Johnson, wives of former Presidents of the United States, were swept in for brief appearances too.

There was great diversity among the delegates. Each woman there was governed by her own spiritual, social, and genetic breeding. Her experiences in life colored her view. This meeting was not convened to enact legislation. The business of the event was largely to hear each other out — though only the few wearing a certain colored ribbon were recognized by the chair. The real opportunity to become acquainted with each other happened informally. And it was valuable. It heightened my awareness of how much work we have to do among today's people.

The delegation from one of the southern states was positioned next to our group. One day I sat next to a black woman who had the same name as mine. We laughed about that because it was about all we had in common. But I cultivated a relationship and nurtured friendship with her for the sake of my Christian principles, for learning and influencing as well, if possible. We both had large families, but the difference was that I knew who the father of my children was and where he was. Our relationship was intact and wholesome. She'd known a parade of men and loved each one in her way. But as to the fathering, who could say?

I had an education, too, and spiritual training that provided me with insights and principles of truth for a better life. She'd not been so advantaged, but she had made the most of an underprivileged life and was there to help improve the lot of scores of other women like herself. She was counting on many changes being wrought in that great hall that week. Little did she understand the forums and frustrations of government.

I watched her vote for every resolution that provided for a government handout of some kind: free day-care centers, stipends for wives of prisoners, total medical care, housing, food stamps, transportation, abortions, contraceptives, and paid vacations, along with quality education.

Finally I said to her: "But how will all of these things you want be paid for? Who will fund the centers, the services, the luxuries across the board that you have voted for?"

Her answer in its entirety was revealing. "Why, honey," she patiently explained, "the United States government!" (Bring me your tired, your poor, your huddled masses. . . . America—land of the brave and giver of all good gifts!)

"Oh, I see," I said. "And where will the United States government get the money?"

"I certainly don't know. That's *their* problem!"

Indeed! And ours as well. I reminded her that taxing us was one way government funds were obtained.

"Then taxes it is!" she exclaimed enthusiastically. "My babies have to be cared for."

It simply was beyond her, these complicated machineries of life. But she knew about loving. She told me she had loved the parade of men in her life, and I'm sure that was true for the level of love she knew about. But her children were her family. She'd fight for their well-being.

Sleepless hours permit the luxury of thinking about people who have been worthy examples of service.

Leicester, England, is in the industrial area of that choice nation. Some years ago my group arrived there, weary from four weeks of solid travel and training. We'd met with youth leaders the evening before and had left early the next morning to cover the distance to the next location.

Our schedule allowed a little free time in Leicester. We had arrived in the early part of the day and didn't have a training session until 7:00 P.M. We were exultant to finally have time to do some laundry and some personal grooming, and to go shopping for a few supplies.

The woman who met us at the hotel was a wonder. She was wreathed in smiles, and though her hands were empty her welcome was warm. She apologized for not having any gifts or any snacks. Times were hard in Leicester. She arranged for our luggage to be stored with the hotel clerk. She informed us that there was not time to go to our rooms, since we had a long jaunt ahead of us to make it to the meeting site. In fact we had long walks, bus trips, and a train ride just to get to the meeting place in the outstretches of the city. She was our guide, and she had to be at the meeting early to get the place ready.

So we left all promise of comfort, rest, and personal pampering, and followed her selfless example with thumbs up.

We made our way down the hill, over the factories, atop the double-deckers, over the bridges, tripping on cobblestones and wading through weeds and creeks. Hours later we came to the ancient meeting hall built of stone for early Christians by some forgotten mason.

She pitched in to fire the stove as the damp hall needed warming. Meanwhile, we chatted about her life. This trek we had just made was what she did several times a week to clean this building, stoke the fire, get the chairs ready, and turn on the electricity for the meetings of the week. For this she was paid a small sum. She was sure that *I* would understand the need for a youth leader to have a little money. Her family funds were limited. She needed to accomplish the Lord's work with the youth. That took money for supplies and treats to keep the young people coming.

I felt ashamed for wanting quiet in a hotel room. I thought of the many Church members in the world who didn't even want to go down the hill or across the street to attend a meeting.

Russia's war memorials are the best part of the city. In Lenigrad, wide plazas and some landscaping soften the scene and attract natives as well as tourists, though if there is any time to loiter the people line up before the beerwagons.

My friend and I walked across one broad plaza in the early morning. Being a lonely grandmother, I was taken by a toddler who was playing while a kerchiefed woman watched. His leggings and hooded jacket were hand-knit and quaint by American standards, I supposed, but I was charmed. I wanted a picture of that little cherub who was the hope of future Russia.

I approached the woman, smiled, showed her my camera, and then pointed to the child. I wanted her permission. She nodded her consent. There were smiles exchanged and the picture was taken. Again I tried to communicate—I put my hand across my heart and bowed slightly, nodding my head and smiling my thanks.

As I turned to follow after my friend, the kerchiefed woman stooped to the child, picked him up, and thrust him toward me. "Amerika! Amerika!" she cried urgently, and as she said the word she handed me the child. I have seldom felt so helpless—nor so privileged. My arms opened in the gesture of helplessness. She understood and lowered that darling boy-child to the ground. It was an act of despair.

What could we do, we two women in a mixed-up world? We looked deep into each other's eyes and understood all this and more. I touched her briefly on the arm and walked away.

Often I dream about the unselfish things people do to help the next generation. I remember a time in Belgium when people from several different countries speaking several different languages crowded into impossible quarters to learn a program to guide young women into loftier paths than ordinary life would permit. There was no sound system and no sound buffer such as carpets or draperies. The room was small, and chairs were placed in every possible corner to accommodate a room bursting with people. But it also was a room bursting with spirit, and that made all the difference.

The women sat in groups of twenty or thirty according to the language they spoke. An interpreter stood before each group. What I was teaching was being translated simultaneously, out loud, in five languages! Babel revisited!

It was the best arrangement possible to overcome barriers. The coordinator of the event was like an eagle to me. He hovered and guarded and worried and inspected, his eyes roving anxiously from group to group. He watched me intently as I spoke, then quickly turned to the various translators and their charges to see if the message was received. His face reflected his caring. He'd frown and mentally reach and root for understanding. He'd spiritually pull for a stumbling translator. He'd smile encouragement at the congregation.

And I thought I had it tough! But that man was perspiring heavily before we were very far into the meeting. He cared so much. What a high place he has in my storehouse of memories to mull over on a sleepless night!

No, he wasn't a hovering eagle. He was more like a very conscientious shepherd.

So was Dame Miriam Dell, who had been honored by the Queen of England and was president of the International Council of Women while I was involved.

We were having a grand gathering of women in Seoul, Korea. I had arranged for a custom gift as a tribute for Dame Miriam. It was a leather-bound book of her life, complete with maps, news clippings, historical data of the places she and her ancestors had lived in—her genealogy back to the fifteenth century in some cases—and excerpts from treasured personal records of her forebears. The only problem was how to give it to her and when. It was an expensive project in terms of money and effort. It was, as far as I was concerned, the ultimate gift, and as much mileage as possible should come from it. Dame Miriam deserved to be recognized, and it was a chance to help some women from the world know about records and genealogy.

I had written a letter in advance of the gathering, asking for a few moments on the schedule—whenever the executive body felt it was appropriate. I explained that the United States of America had a *surprise* tribute to make to Dame Miriam. No response came.

I arrived at the meeting with my gift in hand and spoke personally to Dame Miriam's aides who had control of the agenda. Nothing definite. The days passed and with it numerous opportunities, any one of which I felt would have been a perfect setting for the presentation.

The next to last day of the event arrived. Dame Miriam, of course, knew nothing of my dilemma. But the Lord did. I had prayed fervently for guidance, for doors to be opened. And on that day I prayed for comfort and understanding—it wasn't personal glory I was seeking, not even glory for Dame Miriam. It was an opportunity to remind this gathering of the importance of the family, to turn the hearts of the children to their fathers. I was willing now to do the Lord's will and take my gift back to America and mail it to Dame Miriam. Perhaps

I was the block, not the committee. I asked forgiveness for my arrogance, for my precocious dreams. I prayed, too, that other forces that might block the good that could come from such a presentation and explanation, however brief, would be softened.

And while I was thus on my knees, the telephone in my hotel room rang. My heart was pounding as I answered it. I *knew* that this call was in response to my prayers.

"Cannon?" the woman from Israel, with a coarse voice that seemed to match her nature, asked.

"Yes."

"Good. Tomorrow at the final plenary session you will have fifteen minutes for your presentation. Au revoir."

She hung up without hearing my "Oh, thank you."

I dressed in a white pleated skirt, navy sweater, and red scarf. In my heart I was a stand-in for Miss Liberty! The timing couldn't have been better. I'd only hoped for a brief appearance at the executive sessions, or at a luncheon meeting, perhaps. What God had given was a chance for the Church and America to have center stage—for a moment, but also for the record—at the total gathering. Everybody from every country participating would be there.

When the time came for the presentation, the session was lacking in luster. The meetings had been frustrating and full of quarrels, misunderstandings, and arguments, and reports echoed this. Women trying to help women, according to their own definitions, had bombed. Many were paying no attention to the summaries. And then I was announced.

My legs shook as I moved toward the podium. I was certain I'd be speechless at best and perhaps faint at worst. But I uttered a silent prayer to seal my fast and began my tribute to Dame Miriam. The convention body came to attention as I explained the gift. It had been prepared by The Church of Jesus Christ of Latter-day Saints from their mighty resources of records from around the world. It was presented by the United States of America (and in cooperation with Dame Miriam's daughter who had kept the project a secret) to a woman from New Zealand who had tirelessly served without remuneration or much glory for the universal causes of women—motherhood, health, well-being, education, security, and peace.

But then the magic happened. I leafed through the book and told about Dame Miriam's ancestor being the first Christian missionary in New Zealand. I told about her unusual relationship with her own father and read a letter from him to her. I spoke of her husband, who waited patiently for her return from difficult trips into the places of women across the world. I explained her struggles to attain doctorate degrees while having her babies. I shared personal stories of growth and compassion.

The delegation before me were unified for the first time that week. They laughed. They wept. They understood each other across the barriers of language, color, gods, water supplies, and voting privileges.

Following the meeting a distinguished, handsomely dressed and coiffed woman from France sought me out and summed up the experience for me. "Madam Cannon, I was a girl when the Americans liberated France again during World War II. I wept at those Yanks marching down the streets of a free Paris. My quiet shouts blended with my countrymen in praise to the United States of America. Oh, we worshipped America! . . . But the years passed and we had our differences, your country and mine. I lost my love for America and Americans. But this day, it has returned. America understands what life should be. Thank you for this return to my old, beautiful faith."

"Don't thank me. Thank God," I responded. I held her a moment in my arms and whispered a truth I knew: "Let us each thank God for this day as we pray tonight."

I had another experience that moved me to thank God at bedtime. I was in Israel and was in charge of a bus full of people who had made a sacrifice to visit the Holy Land.

The sleek, new, generously glassed touring bus moved slowly up the steep climb to the sacred mount, that place of peace where the Savior taught the Beatitudes—how people should be with each other.

But there was not peace on our bus. We had an Arab bus driver and a Jewish guide, and they had been fighting their own battle for the last three stops. Obviously, their differences were reaching the point of explosion. In whatever language they were shouting obscenities, I know swearing and threatening by the expression on a man's face and the color of his neck.

Since I was the tour director, I was responsible for the people on my bus. I had come to value our Jewish guide, had been invited into his home to meet his wife and child, had talked gospel with him, and had shared sacred books at his request. And I had good feelings about the bus driver. His dark eyes were warm and his spirit docile. He was truly grateful for treats and kindnesses along the way, as he labored skillfully to get us safely around.

It was all changed now. These two men, like their nations, were at war. Suddenly the guide started giving body punches to the driver. Just as suddenly, the driver spun the huge bus into a horizontal position across the boulevard up the hill of the Beatitudes. A knife was pulled. The passengers cried out and then were silent.

And I was supposed to be in charge!

First, I prayed fast and anxiously, needful and frightened.

Second, I stood up in the aisle next to the angry men now in charging stance, and put my hand on each man's shoulder.

I hoped my touch would electrocute them, but they hardly noticed it. I spoke calmly to them. I spoke firmly, in my best "mother's tone." I put my hands in the prayer position beneath my chin and pleaded.

Then I got smart and showed them my fat wallet with bills for their tips. I threatened them with the promise that there would be no tip. They knew from the days before that this tour's tips were generous.

And that stopped them. Reluctantly they both calmed down. The bus was righted and we went on up the hill. But I was disgusted. The world had come to this. Money was master.

When the Jewish guide finally took his seat for the remainder of the ride up the hill, I moved to sit down by him to explain our feelings. This place was very sacred to all of us on board this bus. It was a pilgrimage of peace, refreshment of soul, and renewal of mind for us. We could not tolerate negative influences. We would not use his services at this spot. We would hold forth on our own.

The work of a licensed Jewish guide is an echo of his ego. It is his worth, his purpose in being. To feel response from his audience and watch tourists on their own steal into the gathering ''at his feet'' was the best part of his profession. To be denied this was a threat, a deep hurt.

My confidence and firmness came from the power of God in me for the good of the people on my bus. I was resolute but I was kind. I also promised the tip only if he kept to this arrangement.

We held our sacred meeting, said our prayer, and sang our songs. We pointed out the differences in the Sermon on the Mount as it is recorded in the Bible and in the Book of Mormon: ''Blessed are the peacemakers for they shall be filled with the Holy Ghost.''

I was startled to look up and see our guide listening intently to us from behind a post a distance away but within earshot. He was subdued, mellow, and ashamed, I think, as we made our way back to the hotel.

Perhaps nothing happened to change the life of a certain guide or a bus driver after all. But it affected me. I see each of those two men clearly and individually. I see them in anger and in peace. When I give thought to them and the eternal problem between their nations, I realize afresh the shallowness of philosophies that leave a man bereft of the hope for peace, that leave a person's soul without light.

If you can't sleep one night, try remembering the times when you have had to be a peacemaker. Count the people on one hand you know who have themselves been peacemakers.

I think of Harry Goulding. Harry was a peacemaker. Oh, how blessed a man was Harry Goulding! He's gone to his generous reward, I'm sure, but while he was still living in *his* Garden of Eden, my husband and I visited him there. For me, it was one of these remarkable turning points that come unbidden in life.

We stayed in his picturesque lodge for invited guests, and one morning Harry loaded a case of canned goods into the Jeep where we waited. We were taking an excursion into the inimitable, mysterious land of the tinted shadows—Monument Valley—on the border of southeastern Utah and northern Arizona. Harry was known as "Mr. Monument Valley" for a season of important years. He was instrumental in getting a Seventh-Day Adventist hospital established there for the local tribe. The Native Americans knew him and trusted him.

He loved them in return and he served them. But his compassion was wise. The hospital helped the Indians in time of sickness, and Goulding's Trading Post kept them solvent, so to speak.

To be shown towering, desert-red monoliths by the inimitable Harry Goulding was to know part of God's country as He created it. And Harry taught us about peace. We'd drive in silence for long stretches across sifting sand. Silence by invitation at first, and then we kept our own peace by choice.

Time then to feel, time to reach back into those clouds of glory we all trailed between heaven and here, time to wonder.

One incident haunts me still.

Harry drove across the pink sand and sandstone, not on a scenic trip this time but searching for little Indian children who were watching their few goats and sheep, protecting the family's precious wealth.

These children would become shepherds on weekdays before they were of school age. They'd be alone for five days at a time, sheltered by miles of sky-high monoliths. And God.

We drove toward two small figures struggling near a watering hole. When we came to a stop, the little shepherdess and her toddler sister were trying to free a goat caught in the cistern. It was a job difficult enough for my husband and Harry, who were quick to help. It was impossible for those children.

The girls were dusty, with disheveled braids and black hair in strands across their faces. But they were beautiful in their Navajo costumes. How they wrenched this mother's heart of mine. I wanted to gather them up and take them home to their place or mine, but Harry cautioned me into calm behavior.

Without a fuss, he went to the case goods box and opened a can of peaches. He indicated, without words, that the big girl was to see that the little sister had her share. There were nods of understanding. They did not grab or gulp. Amazing! The rest of the menu was Vienna sausage and cut green beans. That would be all the real food they would have until Harry came by again. At night they would huddle together, with the lambs and goats, under the shelter of an outcropping of red rock.

Your own adventures are what you may be thinking about when you can't sleep. There are important values to consider from such exposure to other situations, other precious people in Heavenly Father's family.

Remember the rocking chair I told you about that was left in the house down the hill from my childhood home? Well, across the years I came full circle to the truth I'd learned as a child.

I was in the rural reaches of the Philippine Islands. A rocking chair was the sole piece of furniture in a one-room shanty that a fine young family called home. They lived next door to a stunning white church. It was a new church, simple but fully equipped with a modern kitchen and showers for the people getting baptized in the font with new stone steps, which was at the top of a mound. The building and grounds were protected by new chain-link fencing.

As my group visited with this family who lived in poverty in the shadow of plenty, according to my standards, surprisingly love was the overpowering emotion. One might have felt anger or awkwardness about the white church so sequestered and so unavailable to this family. One might have felt pity or even guilt. But not around these people. They were filled with excitement and gratitude that they had such a thing of beauty to look at and to watch over.

Their packing-box home had a dirt floor and a roof of palm fronds. Woven mats hung outside for family sleeping, on nails. There was a single basket for storage and also a rocking chair, which had been left by some missionary.

Unlike my childhood neighbors who felt poor when only a rocker was left, this Filipino family felt rich *because* they had a rocker. They sang for us with their arms wrapped around each other, while the dog wagged its tail. They smiled at each other and at us. And they took turns in the chair, rocking in rhythm as they sang.

While the others were saying good-bye, I stood a moment in that little house with my hands on the back of the rocker. My mind reached back to what then was called our Depression days and the family I knew who had all their furniture but the rocking chair hauled back to the store. How rich they were by comparison to what I was seeing that day!

Mine was an attitude of gratitude for what really counts in life.

Memories. Learnings. James Montgomery wrote something appropriate for those of us who dream a great deal these days and know the meaning of the line, "I'll see you in my dreams . . . ":

> Night is the time to weep;
> To wet with unseen tears
> Those graves of memory,
> Where sleep the joys of other years.

To one who sighs for rest, counting your blessings by the faces of loved ones and beloved strangers who have crossed your life can be wholesome activity until sleep comes.
And good dreaming.

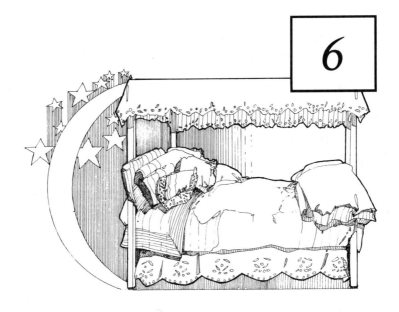

Pillow Talk

I once took the night train to Paris. A remarkable adventure in bedtime activities.

Five other women (according to the porter) and I were stacked three-deep in bunks. We had crept into our corners in the dark and hadn't even seen each other. The quarters were close and so was our breathing. Sleep came hard and in short spans.

Sleeping with strangers is not my idea of a good night's rest.

I stretched fully clothed on my bunk, tucking my purse and passport case firmly in the small of my back.

I stared at the boards of the bunk above me. No sleep.

I couldn't see in the dark, but I was conscious of some person above me, one below me, and three almost within reach across from me. It seemed silly to pretend they weren't there—I could hear them. They weren't asleep either. It seemed unfriendly not to even acknowledge the presence of other human beings.

I whispered a small "Goodnight!" into the dark. Mumbles came back in French and other languages. Miserable as the arrangements were, talking would pass the time at least.

"Anybody else here speak English?" I ventured.

"Oui! Si! Ja! Sure! Mmpf."

"Fine. We're in business. Do you feel like talking?"

"Oui! Si! Ja! Sure! Mmpf."

Good! Inside, people are alike all around the world, even on the night train to Paris that transports all kinds.

Sleeping with strangers is not anybody's idea of a good night's rest.

Since I had generated the pillow talk, I was the self-appointed discussion leader. "Has anyone taken the night train to Paris before?"

"Oui! Si! Ja! Sure! Grunt."

So, I was the only first timer. I said, "This is my first trip. A friend of mine said everyone should take the night train to Paris at least once."

"Yeah? I'd get a new friend if I were you. That one is sick!" An American, who else?

I moved on, directing questions toward each bunk in turn and getting answers in accented English. It was wonderful!

"Bunk above, where is your home?"

"Middle bunk across, what about you? School? Married? Children? Citizenship?"

"Top bunk across, do you work? Where is this train taking you?"

"Lower bunk same side, what are your special interests and talents? Do you have any observations about the gift of life?" Heavy question. Long pause and quiet breathing, waiting.

And then came a gentle, thoughtful response about the innate goodness of people wherever you find them.

Aah! Truth on the night train to Paris.

We pillow-talked each other into comfortable understanding and finally to sleep for a time.

Pillow talk can happen whenever you lie down, sink your head into a pillow, and close your eyes, ready to release the tender feelings of your heart to the right listener.

Pillow talk includes things you can say in the dark but would resist sharing in the bright light of day.

Pillow talk is the kind of talk you can do with God or with yourself about yourself.

Pillow talk can be with the person by your side when you are not in bed but they are, when you're beside the hospital bed of a spouse, or after you have tucked a child in for the night.

What parent hasn't had an experience like this one described in verse by Andrew Gillies?:

> Last night my little boy confessed to me
> Some childish wrong;
> And kneeling at my knee,
> He prayed with tears—
> "Dear God, make me a man
> Like Daddy—wise and strong;
> I know you can."
>
> Then while he slept
> I knelt beside his bed,
> Confessed my sins,
> And prayed with low-bowed head—

"O God, make me a child
Like my child here—
Pure, guileless,
Trusting Thee with faith sincere."

Blessed be the father who prays like that by his child's bedside! Mothers have a place in prayer too. I have felt that the following poem by Carol Lynn Pearson could be labeled "Pillow Talk with God," after the struggle of the day.

On Nest Building

Mud is not bad for nest building.
Mud and sticks
And a fallen feather or two will do
And require no reaching.
I could rest there, with my tiny ones,
Sound for the season, at least.

But—
If I may fly awhile—
If I may cut through a sunset going out
And a rainbow coming back,
Color upon color sealed in my eyes—
If I may have the unboundaried skies
For my study,
Clouds, cities, rivers for my rooms—
If I may search the centuries
For melody and meaning—
If I may try for the sun—

I shall come back
Bearing such beauties
Gleaned from God's and man's very best.
I shall come filled.

And then—
Oh, the nest that I can build!

(Carol Lynn Pearson, from *The Flight and the Nest*
[Salt Lake City: Bookcraft, 1975], title poem.)

The lines below by e. e. cummings delight me. How about writing a few lines for your mother and leaving them on her pillow last thing at night?:

> if there are any heavens my
> mother will (all by herself) have one.
> it will not be a pansy heaven nor
> a fragile heaven of lilies-of-the-valley
> but it will be a heaven of blackred roses.

This book is called *Bedtime Stories for Grownups,* if you recall. Reading good material is what it is all about . . . reading and the ideas it generates.

One of my most precious books—absolutely precious along with the scriptures—is Willa Cather's *My Ántonia.* It's the kind of book I wish I had written, the kind of book I wish more people would read.

It occurs to me that our homes would be richer and our spirits more admirable and content if women, for instance, would spend more time with books (and the people therein) such as *My Ántonia, Precious Bane,* and *The Ponder Heart,* rather than the paperback romance novels and the screamer tabloids at the grocery store check-out points. And that says nothing about prime-time soap operas.

My Ántonia is a noble book about the many heartbeats of love. There is an incident in it that fits in with my notion of good pillow talk, good pillow thinking before sleep takes you away from it all. There are times when it is wonderful to deliberately lie awake considering the lessons learned that day, the mist of memories that touched your heart when, as the following segment portrays, you see someone you used to love. (Used to? Still do!):

> It was eleven o'clock when I at last took my bags and some blankets and started for the barn with the boys. [They] told me to choose my own place in the haymow, and I lay down before a big window, left

open in warm weather, that looked out into the stars. Ambrosch and Leo cuddled up in a hay-cave, back under the eaves, and lay giggling and whispering. They tickled each other and tossed and tumbled in the hay; and then all at once, as if they had been shot, they were still. There was hardly a minute between giggles and bland slumber. . . . I lay awake for a long while, until the slow-moving moon passed my window on its way up the heavens. I was thinking about Ántonia. . . . Ántonia had always been one to leave images in the mind that did not fade—that grew stronger with time. In my memory there was a succession of such pictures. . . .

She was a battered woman now, not a lovely girl; but she still had that something which fires the imagination, could still stop one's breath for a moment by a look or a gesture that somehow revealed the meaning in common things. All the strong things of her heart came out in her body, that had been *so tireless in serving generous emotions.* (From *My Ántonia* by Willa Cather. Copyright 1918 by Willa Sibert Cather. Copyright renewed 1946 by Willa Sibert Cather. Copyright renewed 1954 by Edith Lewis. Reprinted by permission of Houghton Mifflin Company. Italics added.)

"Tireless in serving generous emotions." What a telling phrase!

It happened that while I was reading Ántonia's story again—this time not as a schoolgirl but in my maturity—President Harold B. Lee invited me into his office to talk about the problems people were having in their marriages. He wanted a woman's point of view about the kinds of preparation the Church was providing to people in the developmental stages of life. People needed programs that could ensure happier relationships when they settled down to build a family.

President Lee was a wise man and all he really wanted from me was a sounding board, so I didn't offer much to the conversation, but oh, what I took away!

Among other very important observations that he made was this one: the master bedroom should be the happiest place in the house. It was a sacred place, a meeting place with God. Couples shouldn't go into the bedroom angry. That is where the healing and the soothing happen after all the struggles of the day, and after disturbing matters have been settled amicably, or at least put on the shelf until they can be resolved.

Now, that is wise counsel.

We should try to be more tireless in serving generous emotions. That practical approach to peaceful rest, and thus happier days, had a powerful effect on my personal life and on my teaching of others. Pillow talk is an important idea to me. It is a love-nurturing time. John Donne said:

Love, all alike, no season knows nor clime,
Nor hours, days, months, which are the rags of time.

Pillow talk can cover a lot of subjects, but one thing it should *not* be is argumentative.

Talk of love. And listen . . . listen with love.

There is an old Arabic folk message that has been interpreted or restated by many a poet and author. One of the best renderings is this one by Dinah Maria Mulcock Craik on friendship, which is the better side of any loving relationship:

Oh, the comfort—the inexpressible comfort
Of feeling safe with a person.
Having neither to weigh thoughts,
Nor measure words—but pouring them
All right out—just as they are—
Chaff and grain together—
Certain that a faithful hand will
Take and sift them—
Keep what is worth keeping—
And with the breath of kindness
Blow the rest away.

That poem was given to me, memorized by heart, by my lifelong friend, somewhere in the midyears of our friendship. Sometimes it's easier to be friends when you don't live in the same household. But whether or not you live in the same house or share the same pillow, learning how to love, how to be a friend, is worth the effort. The goal, I suppose, is becoming spiritually so close that one tastes salt when the other one cries—literally or figuratively.

There is a sleeper book on this subject. I say "sleeper" because it has never hit the best-seller list, nor does it meet today's demands for material that ought to be censored—it seems to me, at least. But it is great reading—good plot, developed characterizations, educational, romantic, intriguing.

Precious Bane is a satisfying book for people interested in the great commandments of God that have to do with love, friendship, and the care and keeping of such relationships. This book is a small wonder. It is a novel by Mary Webb which so moved former British Prime Minister Stanley Baldwin that he wrote a glowing introduction to it when it was issued in 1928. The narrative is told by a fifteenth-century Shropshire maiden with a harelip—her precious bane—and how love unfolds for her. We are talking about real love:

> Suddenly, along the quiet road, through the shadows, and through the mist on my own eyelashes, I saw somebody coming. A man, it was. And if there be any meaning in the word as I hanna thought on, let them that read put it in. Let them put the strength and the power, the kindness and the patience, the sternness and the stately righteousness of all good men into that word, and let him wear it. For it was himself, Kester Woodseaves, the maister. . . .
>
> He wore no beard nor whiskers, so you could see the shape and colour and the lines of all his face, which seemed to me to be a face you could never tire of looking on. . . . I wonder if heaven will be thus, a long gazing on

a face you canna tire of, but must ever have one more glimpse. . . .

What did I do, I, that knew his smile was my summer? Why, I got up so hasty that I upset the daffodillies . . . and the jam-pots for flowers, and I ran from the place as if summat was after me. . . .

"Who *be* she?" he says. And even though it be only a passing thought and three words, I'm a flower that knows the sun.

"Why, her be Sarn's sister from away yonder at the mere. Prue Sarn. The woman with the hare-shotten lip. A very queer creature. But it makes 'em queer, you mind, to be born the like of that. . . ."

He said nought, but he went across and picked up my flowers, setting them in the jam-pots man's fashion, a bit clumsy and all thumbs, enough to make you cry with love. I could see from the dark. . . .

"A very neat, tidy figure she's got," he said. And in a minute I knew that he knew I'd heard, and so would ease the wound. Oh, most kind maister, the very marrow of Him that loved the world so dear! (Mary Webb, *Precious Bane* [New York: Modern Library, 1928], pp. 167–69, 173–74.)

The private pleasures of pillow talk include reading poetry with lamps low and spirits at peace. You can renew, refresh, recharge your batteries of love with lines like these:

> They asked me,
> My friends
> Who claim to know my ways
> Do you love him?
> I've never thought
> Do I love him,
> Or love him not?
> What answers come
> From talk of love?
> Cry joy instead.
> Just laugh
> And cry for joy.

That was expressed by a young girl who had just been given her first kiss (peck?) by a young boy who leaped and ran and sang his way down the hill toward home. Little did they know! But it would have to do until the day of very grown-up love when souls meet, not just lips.

Edmund Spenser's tribute to his love is of such quality that every woman would like it to have been dedicated to her:

> You frame my thoughts and fashion me within;
> You stop my tongue and teach my heart to speak;
> You calm the storm that passion did begin . . .

Here's another tribute whose authorship can't be identified—I'm sorry to say, but it may be something you can use one night when sleep doesn't come. (So you are all alone. Well, remember, true love is eternal, so you can dream can't you? No one has said you can't look back in remembrance now and then or forward in hope.):

> Seeing you smile, the furies fail to stay angry.
> Watching you walk, the beggars forget they are hungry.
> Yours is the breath that sets every new leaf aquiver.
> Yours is the grace that guides the rush of the river.
> Yours is the flush and flame in the heart of the flower:
> Life's meaning, its music, its pride and its power.

Pillow talk changes with the years, with love. What school boys giggle about in a hayloft on a summer sleep out will change with young manhood, deepen when they marry, then heighten when they take on spiritual leadership.

And finally, people grow old or ill. But surprisingly, they feel the same inside. Now, that is a fact that may not be fully appreciated until one tackles going downstairs in the mall wearing bifocals, while Glenn Miller's "Moonlight Serenade" comes over the speaker system.

As consolation, let's consider this comfort from Shakespeare:

Let me not to the marriage of true minds
Admit impediments. Love is not love
Which alters when it alteration finds,
Or bends with the remover to remove: . . .
. . . Love's not Time's fool, though rosy lips and cheeks
Within his bending sickle's compass come;
Love alters not with his brief hours and weeks,
But bears it out even to the edge of doom. . . .
(*The Works of William Shakespeare*, Sonnet 116, [New York: Oxford University Press, 1904], p. 1239.)

Following a great general conference of the Church, I worked with Dr. Keith Engar to provide theme, decorations, script, and entertainment at a dinner for leaders of the Church and their spouses.

The last number on the program had been carefully calculated to bring particular pleasure to President Spencer W. Kimball and his popular wife, Camilla. We had invited the baritone Robert Peterson to come and give a lilt of romance to the group. This kind of refreshment was to be a reward for all they had given to others during the days of conference.

For a special touch, I had ordered an armful of yellow roses—Camilla Kimball's favorite—that Bob would present to her at the end of his group of love songs, and he would do it on behalf of her lifelong sweetheart, Spencer, and in tribute to the example they'd been to people.

Listening to "My Cup Runneth O'er with Love," sung by Robert Peterson, is to give love its proper due. It is always one of those rare musical moments when each person is suddenly, with his lover, alone in the universe.

That night Bob sang it just before the presentation of roses. Bob moved people on a musical thread of emotion and memories that was mesmerizing.

I stood at the back watching the audience watch the entertainment. Throughout the evening one of the men had paid special attention to his wife. She was a beautiful woman who, over the years of his service, had been counted as one of the most charming. But she was a victim of illness—apparently the dreaded Alzheimer's disease in its late stages. He had fed her every bite of food. He had touched her lips with the napkin—and sometimes the front of her chic dinner dress to wipe a spill. He kept his arm around her during the entertainment, and was solicitous about her understanding what was going on. By Bob's last note, everyone was as mellow as saucered butter on a warm day.

Even at that it wasn't the high point of the evening for me. Nor was the delight of the Kimballs at the presentation of the roses. It was the kiss that the husband of the stricken woman—that gentle, loving man—leaned over and gave her full on the lips. All of the memories of the happy years were written on his radiant face. She still was loved. She was still capable of eliciting lasting love within him. What a companion she had been to him, with countless pillow talks in homes and hotels wherever he had taken her across the world!

And I watched unabashedly, unbidden tears brimming my eyes. What a lesson of "love alters not!"

The idea, of course, is to live worthy of such love. To cultivate such love. To strive for skills and understanding to achieve such love. What lovely lines pillows can be heir to then!

No romantic pillow talk enrichment would be complete without a bit of Emily Dickinson. But which to choose is the dilemma—the moth kiss; winding the months in balls; don't alter until the hills do?

Not those, but how is this to send you happily off to sleep?:

> The Pedigree of Honey
> Does not concern the Bee —
> A clover, any time, to him
> Is Aristocracy.

Irving Stone has sold millions of copies of his books and touched countless people with lessons from the lives of the great and the famous, who are the core of his works: *The Agony and the Ecstasy, Lust for Life, Clarence Darrow for the Defense, The President's Lady, Immortal Wife,* to mention some.

With dialogue created in some cases, with documentation of facts, and a few liberties taken with history, Stone has brought to life certain star qualities of the children of God. Woven through fascinating accounts of their inimitable contributions are principles and perspectives of life that can be beneficial to others. When it comes so pleasurably cloaked, the guidance is accepted like candy-capsuled medicine.

Pillow talk between a husband and wife can work its own kind of miracles. A wife can whisper ideas into a husband's ear and mind. In a soothing setting the mind and heart of the man can receive them without feeling threatened. She may alert him to the fact that a daughter needs a father's blessing, a son needs a personal interview, a nation needs to be hyped-up with new patriotism, the women of the Church need to "be patted on the head" in public sermons for sharing the load of caring for their families. Depending on the man's office and work, she can gently, lovingly "observe" and offer perspective. He'll mull it over, sleep on it, and awaken with a new version of a good idea that he will call his own. She has done her wifely part, and he goes forth a wiser man for listening and considering.

Jessie and John Fremont had had such a marriage relationship, but there came a period when John's exploring and map charting was set aside for gold digging. Irving Stone weaves a moving tale based on their lives and this particular period, and I have read this segment again and again for my own needs and that of others who have come for help in marriage.

In proportion as they amassed gold, their marriage, that individual entity which was a third being created by their union, had deteriorated into routine. It was no longer something greater than the sum total of the two of them, but rather something less. . . . Their marriage could be a beautiful thing when they were apart for a purpose, such as an expedition; then it could glow with a sustaining light. Geographic separation did not detract from the stature or intensity of the marriage, but separation in ultimate desires, separation in one's conception of the good and valuable life could slash away at the stature of a marriage until this third being which was created by the meeting of two minds and two hearts had died, and there was little left but a husband and a wife. . . .

This could be the profounder tragedy . . . either of the two mates might die, grow weary or calloused with the ideals of their relationship, become indifferent, disillusioned. Yet even when this happened, the other could maintain the marriage by tenderness, sympathy and patience, by hanging grimly on and fighting, by enduring difficult periods; the marriage would maintain its fundamental strength, would come back to robust life when the temporary derangement had passed. One had to refuse to think in terms of disruption or defeat or possible ending: one had to forgive transgressions, have an iron-willed, incorruptible faith in the permanence of the relationship: for a marriage, like a human life, must endure all manner of vicissitude; the weak mortal, the weak relationship went down to destruction at the first ill wind; the stalwart marriage survived all gales, even though sometimes it had to plunge blindly through black and mounting seas.

But if the marriage . . . had slowly crumbled into meaninglessness, then everything was gone . . . [even if the] plight was no one's fault, but rather a piling up of accidental circumstance. Yet accidental circumstance must not be allowed to be the master, or their lives would be buffeted by every changing wind. (Irving Stone, *Immortal Wife: The Biographical Novel of Jessie Benton Fremont* [Garden City, New York: Doubleday and Company, Inc., 1944], pp. 272–73.)

When you have been married a long, long time, you have earned the right to be a little smug, along with being enormously grateful that your crown is shining, studded with off-spring, and rimmed round with nuggets of little victories over stunning blows. Perhaps you'll understand what Ralph Waldo Emerson says about "green fruit." And for your information, he wrote this when he was about 46—just "over the hill," they say:

"Love is temporary and ends with marriage. Marriage is the perfection which loved aimed at, ignorant of what it sought. Marriage is a good known only to the parties,—a relation of perfect understanding, aid, contentment, possession of themselves and of the world,—which dwarfs love to green fruit."

One doesn't whisper love in pillow talks just to build reciprocal self-esteem. One builds esteem for the institution of marriage and family. One doesn't resist buffeting by changing winds, it seems to me, but, keeping that resolve as a firm goal, moves beyond to curry love, comfort, well-being. Life is eternal, that's why.

It may not matter if over the years of becoming older one also becomes increasingly crotchety, picky, nagging, dissatisfied, and filled with self-pity, wearing a martyr's crown. But since Christianity assures us that every individual is going to go on living, always and forever, what we are becoming makes a big difference. No one wants to live forever with a grouch, a sinner, an insensitive and self-serving partner. It's bad enough to struggle for an hour in such a relationship. And we are rapidly becoming what we are going to be. Such a thought reminds us that as we grow older we ought to be growing up, more like God, the ultimate example. And marriage is the mighty classroom.

Come, now, even if it is the end of the day it is not the end of life. Even if it is the last of the stress-struggle for a few hours, there is no promise that there won't be more tomorrow. We let ourselves age unnecessarily if we can't laugh—if we don't laugh. And if we laugh and love, if we feel vibrations for someone beyond ourselves, we can note that clouds today are different from yesterday, and that even the moon is reflecting more light this week than last. Oh, if we can feel God in us, counting our joy as full (well, almost), then the lines in the face will soften, the twinkle will shine up our eyes, and our voice will carry a lilt.

Let's laugh before bedtime tonight.

> You child, how can you dare complain
> That you and I may be mismated
> Because, you say, you lack a brain
> And I'm so highly educated.
>
> . . . .
>
> We're equal partners, that is plain.
> Our life cannot grow dull or shoddy,
> While I have such a lovely brain,
> And you have such a lively body.
> (Louis Untermeyer from *Men and Women: The
> Poetry of Love* [New York: American Heritage
> Press, 1970].)

This first and last stanza of "Equals" by Louis Untermeyer, gives the message of the compensation of love. The full poem is included in a wide collection of poems on love.

Just a thought or two on the subject of being in love and being alone:

So we are self-reliants.
For example, I had a marvelous day today,
And I didn't even see you.
But how will
Tough
Strong
Thrifty
Brave
And reverent me
Get through tonight?

There is a giving beyond giving
Yours to me
Who awoke last night
Hours before the dawn
Set free
By one intolerable lightning stroke
That ripped the sky—
To understand what love withholds in love
And why.

I don't know who wrote these lines. I've had them memorized since I had to give up a certain grand passion of mine a hundred years ago it seems. But if you know anyone suffering from unrequited love . . .

I met Paul Engle when he was guest lecturing at a seminar for writers, and I wanted to rush up and express my gratitude to him for embodying a universal feeling in language worth memorizing. But I was reticent, and now I am sorry. For why shouldn't we tell the writer about our joy in his words and the emotion that evoked it? He wrote:

Finding you, unexpectedly, in that room
Was more than a mere person in love could stand:
As if on a summer day in the dazzle of noon
One snowflake fell on my astonished hand.

Pillow talk is the time to build, to pay tribute, to count value, to comfort hurts, to reassure, to offer hope and promise, to fulfill as it comes within the possibilities of personal power.

In Proverbs 4:23 is a key so golden it opens the doors of fullness of joy, of choice relationships guided by God's love: ''Keep thy heart with all diligence; for out of it are the issues of life.''

For many years Mother was in charge of the weekly book reviews at the Lion House Social Center, and her collection of books and beautiful messages of love, inspiration, and noble behavior have enriched my life beyond my ability to give thanks for. I first read the following folktale in a very old book in my mother's personal library. It is about ''keeping thy heart with diligence,'' which to me means treating other people as they deserve to be treated, since they, too, are children of God.

Two friends lived on adjoining lands—one alone, and the other with his wife and children. They harvested their grain. One night the man without a family awoke and looked on his sheaves stacked beside him.

''How good God has been to me,'' he thought, ''but my friend with his family needs more grain than I.'' So he carried some of his store to his friend's field.

And the other surveying his own harvest thought: ''How much I have to enrich my life. How lonely my friend must be with so little of this world's joys.''

So he arose and carried some of his grain and placed it on his friend's stack.

And in the morning when they went forth to glean again, each saw his heap of sheaves undiminished.

This exchange continued until one night in the moonlight the friends met, each with his arms filled on the way to the other's field. At the point where they met, the legend says, *a temple was built.*

Here is philosophy that gives direction and value to two people lying side by side at bedtime. Not every night, however carefully calculated, is frosting on the day. There are times when pillow talk is impossible—out of either joy or pain. But there is a paragraph in Ann Morrow Lindbergh's *Gift from the Sea* that I must have shared with a score of couples in pain, who were suffering needless estrangement because "things haven't turned out exactly as they planned" when they got married. Maybe there is someone you'd like to give a copy to. Personally, I think Mrs. Lindbergh was an inspired woman. I find her perspective in keeping with God's truth:

> When you love someone you do not love them all the time, in exactly the same way, from moment to moment. It is an impossibility. It is even a lie to pretend to. And yet this is exactly what most of us demand. We have so little faith in the ebb and flow of life, of love, of relationships. We leap at the flow of the tide and resist in terror its ebb. We are afraid it will never return. We insist on permanency, on duration, on continuity; when the only continuity possible, in life as in love, is in growth, in fluidity—in freedom, in the sense that the dancers are free, barely touching as they pass, but partners in the same pattern. The only real security is not in owning or possessing, not in demanding or expecting, not in hoping, even. Security in a relationship lies neither in looking back to what it was in nostalgia, nor forward to what it might be in dread or anticipation, but living in the present relationship and accepting it as it is now. For relationships, too, must be like islands. One must accept them for what they are here and now, within their limits —islands, surrounded and interrupted by the sea, continually visited and abandoned by the tide. One must accept the security of the wingéd life, of ebb and flow, of intermittency. (From *Gift from the Sea*, by Anne Morrow Lindbergh. Copyright © 1955 by Anne Morrow Lindbergh. Reprinted by permission of Pantheon Books, a division of Random House, Inc.)

To learn to love through ebb and flow is where gospel principles can help us. We can learn from the teachings and example of Jesus, the small moments of miracles that healed the flesh or the soul. To learn this kind of love is reward for the effort. It is eternal life, and meanwhile it opens the door for happy pillow talking.

Edwin Markham said, "Whoever falls from God's right hand is caught into his left." That's a comforting mental picture. Inspired by that and a remembrance that we are to help the Lord Jesus in his mission of making full joy possible for all men who will accept this gift—thinking upon that, this poem of love, also written by Markham, is one I have cherished since my young love days. It gives an added perspective to how people in love should help each other:

Ultimate Love

> I dare not ask your very all:
> I only ask a part.
> Bring me—when dancers leave the hall—
> Your aching heart.
> Give other friends your lighted face,
> The laughter of the years:
> I come to crave a greater grace—
> Bring me your tears!

Aah! Mmmmm!

Though most of us grown-ups don't frequent dance halls much any more, the message of "Ultimate Love" can work for pillow talk times just as well. Compassion, surely, has a place there.

The more we work at good loving, the more we finally are rewarded by growth in our own capacity to love. Ours it is to love.

As old Ben Franklin taught: "If you want to be loved, be loveable."

Another lesson about love: beauty is in the eyes of the one who loves, and that may be the choice miracle in this God-given emotion. One man's sigh is another fellow's ho-hum, but what counts is how our own lover sees us.

There was one month to go in one of my pregnancies, and I looked every inch of it! It was during the period when starched shirts and pinafores were touted as virtuous. I was not only poking out in front but I was also behind in my ironing. In spite of soaring temperatures I was doing my duty— ironing. Perspiration matted my hair, dampened the pinafore, washed my upper lip, and dripped from my wrists so that I could hardly keep a grip on the iron. And besides, since I couldn't get close to the ironing board I looked like a mother kangaroo in a brush fire. Awkward. Hot. Fussed.

Then my husband came home for lunch as a nice surprise. Men!

He smiled when he saw me and said, "You look great!" (He likes me when I'm domestic.) Then he walked right over and hugged me—like Jesus, who said that if we'd keep his counsel he would "encircle us in the arms of [his] love!" What more could anyone ask?

Well, my husband hugged me and hugged me while I sobbed. I knew I didn't look great. I knew I had lost my composure. I knew I'd have to launder and starch and iron his shirt that I was ruining with my tears. But he just went on hugging, murmuring, silencing me in his special way.

That was a hundred years or so ago, and it is a memory that surfaces when I need it most. Granted, it wasn't a bedtime incident, but it set the stage for satisfying pillow talk that night. But there is more: I learned that just being loved is enhancing.

My family and I were new in a neighborhood, and I had just met a fine gentleman with whom I'd be serving in a Church assignment. We were visiting in the foyer of the chapel when I asked him when I would get to meet his wife.

"Now," he said. "Why wait? You are in for a treat!"

"Wonderful," I returned. "Where is she?"

"She's in the cultural hall."

So were a dozen other women I didn't know yet, who were decorating for a church bazaar.

"How will I know her?"

"Easy!" He was exuberant. "Go in there and look for the most beautiful woman in the room—that's my wife." Then he gave me a few more details and I left. I entered the room looking for a lady who was a cross between Sophia Loren and a young Audrey Hepburn. What I saw were mothers of many, empty-nesters, and some fine Molly Mormons. I didn't see one who answered his descriptions at all. Finally I asked someone and she pointed out the man's wife.

As I think about this woman now, I can think only of beauty and loveliness. Honestly. I know her as one of the finest women I've ever met. I love her for her great kindness to me over the years. But at that moment I was shocked. There must be some mistake! Not only was the woman who had been pointed out to me no movie star but she also had few redeeming features. I noticed that she had gentle curls of fine mahogany hair, a light in her eyes, and a warm smile. But that was it. Her eyes were unusually wide set. Her lips were thick, surrounding an ugly overbite. Her ears were prominent. Her nose, however, was the nose of a movie-star— Bop Hope! But that smile and those eyes, when I introduced myself, obliterated imperfect features.

Of course he loved her. He'd lived with her. He'd shared pillow talk. She had been told that she was beautiful and desirable so many times that *she was!* He'd been the object of her incredibly generous service and her unequivocal support. That woman would crawl through a forest of prickly trees and tangleweeds to help her man. Of course he loved her.

The secret of satisfying, sleep-inducing pillow talk might be found in countless kind deeds that people do for each other. At the top of the list is the prayer: "Dear God, help me, an imperfect person, be patient with her/him while she/he grows in perfection."

Meanwhile, make that pillow talk believable. It works wonders.

The idea is to live worthy of the endless love, unaltered love, blind love. Cultivate such love. Strive for skills and understanding to achieve such love. What lovely lines the pillows at bedtime will be heir to then!

Marta, wife of noted cellist Pablo Casals, was always in the wings at his concerts. People remarked at her devotion on all occasions. He was on the stage most of the time, but she was always in the wings. They had worked out their relationship and their responsibilities so that each was fulfilled. A poem was written and dedicated to them by the Puerto Rican poet To'mas Blanco. He was impressed with their love affair year after year, difficulty after difficulty. You might memorize it for some pillow talk of your own:

> See in the waves of the sea
> How much I love you.
> I love you from the depths of my sleeplessness . . .
> I love you beyond space and time.
> I love you . . . I love you.

What do we live for, after all and all, if not to make life more satisfying for each other? Less difficult if we can, but certainly more pleasant.

I bought a bookmark along with a new book the other day. I bought it for the message rather than needing it for a page marker. I have plenty of cardboard bookmarks. I have some as well in brass, silver, embroidery floss and cross-stitch, needlepoint, felt, leather, ribbon, and braided twine. Don't you, too? But this new bookmark is important to me because of the following truth printed on it:

> After a while you learn the difference between holding a hand and chaining a soul. You learn that love isn't leaning but lending support. You begin to accept your

defeats with the grace of an adult, not the grief of a child. You decide to build your roads on today, for tomorrow's ground is too uncertain. You help someone plant a garden instead of waiting for someone to bring you flowers. You learn that God has given you the strength to endure and that you really do have worth. (Anonymous)

"Anonymous" in this case is so sad. I wish I knew who wrote those words—who knew enough about the gentle mosaic of life to write those words. Not just for a "where credit is due" courtesy, but because there is much to learn from such a wise soul.

There is application about loving well in the biblical story of the beggar asking alms of Peter and James at the temple gate. Peter was filled with compassion and looked upon the man and said: "Silver and gold have I none; but such as I have give I thee: In the name of Jesus Christ of Nazareth rise up and walk" (Acts 3:6).

Peter didn't leave it at that, either. He gave the blessing in love, but then he sweetened it with action by taking the beggar by the right arm and lifting him up. Now, whether we are loved in exactly the way we had in mind, it is up to us to accept the gift and the giver—what the giver is capable of giving according to his or her background, qualities, training, and growth. We may not have silver or gold (beauty? charm? money? patience? brains?), but we are loyal, long-suffering, helpful, serving, et cetera, et cetera, et cetera.

From the scriptures comes the highest example of unequivocal and all-encompassing love—the answer to better sleep by night and better life by day:

Though I speak with the tongues of men and of angels, and have not charity, I am become as sounding brass, or a tinkling cymbal. And though I have the gift of prophecy, and understand all mysteries, and all knowledge; and though I have all faith, so that I could remove mountains, and have not charity, I am nothing. And though I bestow all my goods to feed the poor, and though I give my body to be burned, and have not charity, it profiteth me nothing. Charity suffereth long, and is kind; charity envieth not; charity vaunteth not itself, is not puffed up, doth not behave itself unseemly, seeketh not her own, is not easily provoked, thinketh no evil; rejoiceth not in iniquity, but rejoiceth in the truth; beareth all things, believeth all things, hopeth all things, endureth all things. Charity never faileth. . . . (1 Corinthians 13:1–8.)

In Luke 10:27 are these words worth committing to memory and making a part of daily life. They are given to us as a commandment. They preface the parable of the good Samaritan so that they supply a memorable example for understanding.

"Thou shalt love the Lord thy God with all thy heart, and with all thy soul, and with all thy strength, and with all thy mind; and thy neighbour as thyself."

We have learned, too, that we shouldn't just love our friendly neighbors, but we should love our enemies because they, too, are God's children. And because he has commanded it. We also are to love those people who live in the same house with us, who count as family on the records of life.

Now, that is something for parents to talk to their children about when they tuck them in—command them to love each other all the days of their lives that your family may be a unit to stand in love before God.

Pillow talk can change lives, as well as put people to sleep nicely.

Pillow talk can soften and soothe the crumpled spirit.

Pillow talk, remember, can happen wherever you put your head down, whether it is on the night train to Paris, at the cabin in the sky, or in the pullout sleeper in your married kids' family room.

Successful pillow talk takes only a little preparation—you know, just gather a little honey for the hive. The precious moments before bedtime can be the best part of the day. Making an effort to enrich the life and sweeten the sleep of a loved one—child or grown-up—seems to me to be a worthwhile project.

And then, when at last you come to the end of a perfect day (or a perfectly rotten one), you'll have something distracting, something relaxing, something healing, something humorous to talk about.

That's it, just read a little, talk a little, listen to each other plenty, and drop off to sleep, feeling healed and full of joyful expectations for the morrow.

Now snuggle into that pillow and drift off into a good night.

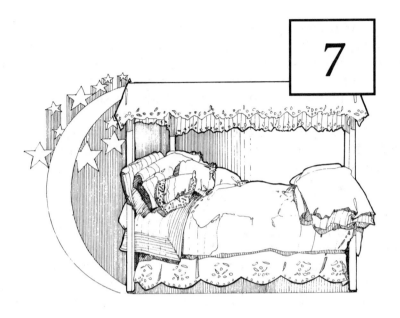

With Your Eyes Wide Open

Do you know what *pervigilium* means? It means with your eyes wide open. Insomnia. Burdened with troubles and bothered by the mysteries, you suffer what Sir Thomas Wyatt called "wakey nights."

The best sleep-inducing procedure for bedtime and one that makes waking up a time of anticipation for the day ahead —the secret to the good life, if you will—is to think upon

God. With your eyes wide open, thinking upon God last thing at night and first thing in the morning is wisdom, comfort, and fruitfulness. Having your eyes wide open by choice is quite different from suffering pervigilium!

Let us move gently down the tides of sleep, of sleep so sound that darkness seems short. And one way to do that is to keep your eyes wide open and to think upon God, the Creator, he who made us and who understands our need for sweet sleep, rest for body, mind, and soul.

I believe in God. I know there is a living God of patience, justice, mercy, and incredible generosity. I believe in a God who understands where we have been (and why) as well as where we are. I believe in a God who stands by us in our struggles and in our delightful times of exploring life. I believe that even darkest tragedy can be faced with equanimity—that we can flourish, not merely survive—when we know God, when we understand his will. The journey through the adventure of life, is enhanced when we pursue the commands Jesus emphasized: ''Learn of me!'' ''Come unto me!'' ''Come, follow me!'' I have listed these calls in a logical order for accomplishment. One learns of Christ and is then naturally drawn to him. One wants to come unto him and communicate with him. The natural outcome of such devotion is to try to follow him, to be like him, and to do as he does. The nicest thing to think about just before being carried away by the miracle of sleep—the unconsciousness from which a person can readily be awakened—is the nature of God and how we can conform our lives to his.

When I was a college girl, I attended a religion class where the teacher quoted from W. P. Montague, who said that it was helpful to happiness to believe in God. Good and bad behavior didn't seem to be the issue. It was not that atheism necessarily led to badness but to "an incurable sadness."

I have thought about that countless times over the years as I've grown in understanding about life, opportunity, self, and God.

If we do not believe in God, if we do not actively appreciate that there is a governing, wiser power than our own selves or any other person on earth, then we are deprived of the richness life can offer. The greatest talent, the kindest deeds, the most beautiful scenery, the highest moments of shared affection would be at the mercy of chance forces. It would be a rampant world marked by menacing unrestraint.

Thank God for God! No such cataclysmic tragedy is ahead for us. Man is eternal, with God. God's principles are so high that we must reach to fully comprehend them, but they rule—no matter who believes or doesn't believe.

In God we find our ideal in whom to "live, and move, and have our being." This faith is what soothes us to sweetest sleep.

> The Lord by wisdom hath founded the earth; by understanding hath he established the heavens.
>
> By his knowledge the depths are broken up, and the clouds drop down the dew.
>
> My son, let not them depart from thine eyes: keep sound wisdom and discretion:
>
> So shall they be life unto thy soul, and grace to thy neck.
>
> Then shalt thou walk in thy way safely, and thy foot shall not stumble.
>
> *When thou liest down, thou shalt not be afraid: yea, thou shalt lie down, and thy sleep shall be sweet.*
>
> Be not afraid of sudden fear, neither of the desolation of the wicked, when it cometh.
>
> For the Lord shall be thy confidence, and shall keep thy foot from being taken. (Proverbs 3:19–26; italics added.)

In a certain segment of that remarkable best-seller *City of Joy*, by Dominque LaPierre, Stephan, the lead character, on his first night in the slums of India, studied his most prized personal possession—the only thing he had brought along with him on his pilgrimage, this self-imposed mission among some of God's children. It was a gift from his father, a photograph of the sacred shroud of Turin. The face of the crucified Christ imprinted on his shroud took on new meaning for him that first evening. It seemed to be the very incarnation of all the martyrs of the slum that he had seen so far. For Stephan, a committed believer, each one of them wore that same expression, that same face of Jesus Christ proclaiming to humanity from the heights of Golgotha all the pain, but also the hope of man rejected. Said Stephan: ". . . That was the reason for my coming. I was there because of the cry of the crucified Christ: I thirst." He had come to give a voice to the hunger and thirst for justice of those who here mounted the cross each day and who knew how to face that death which we in the West no longer know how to confront without despair. Nowhere else was that icon (the shroud) more in its rightful place than in that slum.

Stephan Kovalski pinned up the picture with the aid of two matches stuck in the pisé wall. After a while he tried to pray, but his efforts were in vain. He was dazed. He needed some time to adjust to his new incarnation. As he was pondering, a little girl appeared on the threshold, barefoot and dressed in rags, but with a flower in the end of her pigtail. She was carrying an aluminum bowl full of rice and vegetables. She set it down in front of Kovalski, joined her hands in the Indian gesture of greeting, bowed her head, smiled, and ran away. "I gave thanks to God for this apparition and for this meal provided by brothers unknown to me. Then I ate, as they do, with my fingers. In the depths of this hovel, I felt everything was assuming a very distinctive dimension. So it was that my fingers' contact with the rice made me understand that first night how much the food was not a dead thing, not something neutral, but rather a gift of life." (*City of Joy* [Garden City, New York: Doubleday, Inc., 1985], pp. 60–61.)

How others believe and how they express their feelings on the matter of God's reality can be instructive, heartening, and strengthening to our own increased understanding of the nature of God.

Henry Eyring's blend of science and religion motivated many a young person to set aside time for the study of Deity. Dr. Eyring felt that the study of God and his gospel was the eternal quest for ultimate reality.

There is no question but that the more the world changes, the more it is the same, according to the greatest scientific minds. They, as well as religious thinkers, admit to a higher power, to an orderliness, and to an eternal nature of all creation.

Dr. Eyring was a brilliant and honored scientist in his own right. He spent nearly ten years at Princeton University when Einstein was there at the Institute for Advanced Study. Dr. Eyring writes the following:

"On one occasion when I was with Professor Einstein he expressed interest in the ethical teachings of Confucius but was not particularly interested in the doctrinal teachings of the religions with which he was acquainted. Although he was very loyal to the Jewish people and was a Zionist, he had lost interest in the religious practices of Judaism. In spite of this he was devoutly religious."

Once the men were riding in a car towards Einstein's home, and Dr. Eyring explained to the renowned scientist the Latter-day Saint belief in a preexistence. Professor Einstein immediately asked about the preexistence of animals. Dr. Eyring reported: "I explained our belief that everything was created spiritually before its temporal existence. This interested him. . . . Later, addressing a conference on science, philosophy and religion Einstein said that belief in regularity in nature to which he subscribes belongs to religion . . . ; to this sphere of religion there also belongs the faith in the possibility that the regulations valid for the world of existence are rational, that is, comprehensible to reason. I cannot conceive of a genuine scientist without that profound faith. This situation may be expressed by an image: science without religion is lame, religion without science is blind.''

To Einstein there had to be a higher power. Dr. Eyring went on to suggest that he personally had known some first-rate scientists who were agnostic, but that experience would indicate that among distinguished physical scientists the percentage who ''believe in a Supreme Being is higher than in the population at large. . . . The Latter-day Saint belief in a pre-existence with existence continuing on into eternity seems the natural destiny of the human soul with its limitless potentialities.''

''Limitless potentialities'' indeed! What an idea to dwell upon, lying quietly in a clean bed. To rest in quiet darkness, to ponder the powers of God and the stretch of the human soul, and then at last to sleep upon such thoughts, that is the ideal way to move into the hours set aside for sleep.

I've lived long enough now to make some safe comparisons. The old movies and the old books by and large are the best sources for additional perspective on faith, God, life after death, and the wholesome way to pursue life. My husband and I have a fine library of old movies and old books as well as current publications and videos. The experiences of Dr. Eyring with Dr. Einstein would have escaped me entirely, if I had not leafed through an old book about scientists and God.

Some public writers today seem to be untrained in an understanding of God, and therefore lacking in knowledge of such important truth, or perhaps they are simply reticent to admit their need of a higher power. One can have hope that there is a caring God but not have an understanding of his nature or even conviction of his existence.

It does not seem to be chic today in the media to declare belief in God. God is merely an expletive.

But John D. Rockefeller, Jr., believed in God. He said so in big stone and brass in a public center in New York City, built by the Rockefeller millions. John D. mounted his statement of ten truths under the title "I Believe." The last two items are these:

"I believe in an all-wise and all-loving God, named by whatever name, and that the individual's highest fulfillment, greatest happiness, and widest usefulness are to be found in living in harmony with His will.

"I believe that love is the greatest thing in the world; that it alone can overcome hate; that right can and will triumph over might."

Last Christmas my great friend and brother brought me a little treasure. Books are always the choice gift of the season, and this gift he had found during a favorite activity of his— browsing in a used book store as a respite between sessions over which he presided in court.

He had been impressed by this book as a young man when working out his personal beliefs about God. He found this 1918 copy—printed before I was born—and I was delighted to be introduced to it. It is Harry Emerson Fosdick's *The Meaning of Faith*. The following enlightenment to read before slipping into slumber is excerpted from the first chapter, "Faith and Life's Adventure":

Man's life, interpreted and motivated by religious faith, is glorious, but shorn of faith's interpretations life loses its highest meaning and its noblest hopes. Let us make this statement's truth convincing in detail.

When faith in God goes, man the thinker loses his greatest thought. . . . Amid the crash of stars, the reign of law, the vicissitudes of human history, and the griefs that drive their plough-shares into human hearts, to gather up all existence into spiritual unity and to believe in God, is the sublimest venture of the human mind.

When faith in God goes, man the worker loses his greatest motive. To believe that we do not stand alone, hopelessly pitted against the dead apathy of cosmic forces which in the end will crush us . . . bring our work to naught . . . to believe that we are fellow-laborers with God, our human purposes comprehended in a Purpose, God behind us, within us, ahead of us—this incomparably has been the master-faith in man's greatest work.

When faith in God goes, man the sinner loses his strongest help. . . . He is the only creature whom we know whose nature is divided against itself. . . . That God himself is pledged to the victory of righteousness in men and in the world, that he cares, forgives, enters into man's struggle with transforming power. . . . Such faith alone [is] great enough to meet the needs of man the sinner.

When faith in God goes, man the mortal loses his only hope. . . . Whoever discards religious faith should appoint a day of mourning for his soul, and put on sackcloth and ashes . . . they . . . indict their own intelligence. . . . We know that something is now ours which ought not to die; the instinct of an unknown continent burns in us. But all the hopes, the motives, the horizons that immortality has given man must go, if faith in God departs. In a godless world man dies forever. . . . Before one thus leaves himself bereft of the faith that makes life's adventure most worthwhile he well may do what Carlyle, under the figure of Teufelsdröckh, says that he did in his time of doubt: "In the silent night-watches, still darker in his heart than over sky and hearth, he has cast himself before the Allseeing, and with audible prayers cried vehemently for Light." (*The Meaning of Faith* [New York: Association Press, 1918].)

It's true in each of our lives that situations and influences can alter our faith, strengthening it or causing us to question its essential meaning. There is one incident from scripture that always is relevant to the matter of faith. It is centered in the ministry of Elijah at which time the prophets of Baal were having some success with the people. The challenge he made echoes in our hearts today: "And Elijah came unto all the people, and said, How long *halt ye between two opinions?* if the Lord be God, follow him: but if Baal, then follow him. . . ." Through a series of remarkable events Elijah overcame the prophets of Baal. Elijah proved to the people that the Lord was God, and "they fell on their faces: and they said, The Lord, he is the God; the Lord, he *is* the God." (1 Kings 18:21, 39; italics added.)

Sleepless nights might be a perfect time to think upon what we know to be true and how we can implement such truth in our lives. To consider what is true and then to live by that truth proves us wise. To claim to know truth and then not to adhere to it proves us foolish.

Many have asked, What is God like? I think of phrases such as these: "I will lead thee by the hand and give thee answer to thy prayers." "Draw near unto me, and I will draw near unto you." "Ask, and ye shall receive." "I, the Lord, am bound when ye do what I say." "I will encircle you in the arms of my love." "Behold I am Jesus Christ!"

Tennyson said it in this way:

> Flower in the crannied wall,
> I pluck you out of the crannies,
> I hold you here, root and all, in my hand,
> Little flower—but if I could understand
> What you are, root and all, and all in all,
> I should know what God and man is.

It has been the business of prophets over the generations to help people see what God and man are.

When Elder Ezra Taft Benson, then a member of the Quorum of the Twelve and the United States Secretary for

Agriculture, was visiting Russia, he was allowed to visit the Central Baptist Church in Moscow. He was deeply moved by the devoted, poverty-stricken old people in attendance. They were the only Russian generation alive who had been taught to believe in God. As a distinguished visitor and United States government official, he had the opportunity to speak to them. He spoke about hope and truth and love, and as he did so, tears flowed freely on the faces of the congregation and the members of the press and security who accompanied him. Surely not only because of the words he spoke but also because of the Spirit accompanying the speaker.

Ezra Taft Benson testified: "Our Heavenly Father is not far away. He is our Father. Jesus Christ watches over this earth. He is the Redeemer of the world. Be unafraid. Keep his commandments. Love one another. Pray for peace. And all will be well."

Janet Palmer, after thirty years in the English department, was given a well-deserved honorary doctorate from Westminster College. I'd like to drum up an award of my own to bestow upon her just for bringing to my attention these lines from Robert Browning's "Ulysses":

> . . . Yet all experience is an arch where thro'
> Gleams that untravell'd world whose margin fades
> For ever and for ever when I move. . . .
>
> Tho' much is taken, much abides: and tho'
> We are not now that strength which in old days
> Moved earth and heaven, that which we are, we are, —
> On equal temper of heroic hearts,
> Made weak by time and fate, but strong in will
> To strive, to seek, to find, and not to yield.
> (Robert Browning, from *Masterpieces of Religious Verse*
> [New York and Evanston: Harper and Row, 1948], p. 283.)

President David O. McKay was on a world tour, and while traveling by train he saw an exquisite sunset. He made a record of it and then wrote the following in his personal journal:

Pondering still upon this beautiful scene, I lay in my berth at ten o'clock at night, and thought to myself: Charming as it is, it doesn't stir my soul with emotion as do the innocent lives of children, and the sublime characters of loved ones and friends. Their beauty, unselfishness, and heroism are after all the most glorious!

I then fell asleep, and beheld in vision something infinitely sublime. In the distance I beheld a beautiful white city. Though far away, yet I seemed to realize that trees with luscious fruit, shrubbery with gorgeously tinted leaves, and flowers in perfect bloom abounded. . . . I then saw a great concourse of people approaching the city. Each one wore a white flowing robe, and a white headdress. Instantly my attention seemed centered upon their Leader, and though I could see only the profile of his features and his body, I recognized him at once as my Savior. The tint and radiance of his countenance were glorious to behold. There was a peace about him which seemed sublime—it was divine!

The city, I understood, was his. It was the City Eternal; and the people following him were to abide there in peace and eternal happiness. But who were they? . . . *"These are they who have overcome the world —who have truly been born again!"*

"When I awoke, it was breaking day over Apia harbor." (Clare Middlemiss, comp., *Cherished Experiences* [Salt Lake City: Deseret Book Co., 1955], pp. 108–10.)

The stories of the prophets of old times and of those of recent days concerning their witness of God are thrilling. A choice bedtime story for a very grown-up disciple of Christ to think about before dropping off to sleep is this one about Lorenzo Snow. It is related by Allie Young Pond, his granddaughter, and is recorded in *Revelation*, by Lewis J. Harmer:

One evening when I was visiting Grandpa Snow in his room in the Salt Lake Temple, I remained until the doorkeepers had gone and the night-watchman had not yet come in, so Grandpa said he would take me to the main, front entrance and let me out that way. He got his bunch of keys from his dresser.

After we left his room and while we were still in the large corridor, leading into the celestial room, I was walking several steps ahead of Grandpa when he stopped me, saying: "Wait a moment, Allie. I want to tell you something. It was right here that the Lord Jesus appeared to me at the time of the death of President Woodruff". . . .

Then Grandpa came a step nearer and held out his left hand and said, "He stood right here, about three feet above the floor. It looked as though he stood on a plate of solid gold."

Grandpa told me what a glorious personage the Savior is and described his hands, feet, countenance, and beautiful white robes, all of which were of such a glory of whiteness and brightness that he could hardly gaze upon him. Then Grandpa came another step nearer me and put his right hand on my head and said: "Now granddaughter, I want you to remember that this is the testimony of your grandfather, that he told you with his own lips that he actually saw the Savior here in the temple and talked with him face to face." (From Lewis J. Harmer, *Revelation* [Salt Lake City: Bookcraft, 1957], pp. 119–20.)

Oh, yes! God lives!

What a pleasant, comforting note that knowledge is to fall asleep on! There can be no ultimate harm, no lasting misery when we know this. Restlessness can be assuaged by turning one's thoughts to Deity.

To all you who suffer from *pervigilium*, try getting your testimony strengthened and all will be well, through the night and always.

Good night.

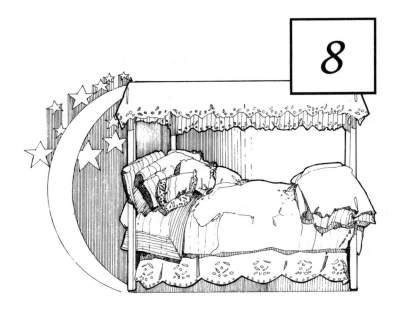

Lullaby and Goodnight

lul-la-by used to lull a child: a soothing refrain; specif: a song to quiet children or lull them to sleep; to quiet with.

We can agree with that official definition, I suppose, and not feel insulted that we choose to talk about lullabies in a book for grown-ups. The child in all of us is seldom so evident as at restless bedtimes. We want to be comforted, calmed, stroked, patted, back-rubbed, tucked in, swathed in our favorite down comforter, and kissed goodnight.

If we can work it right, we also enjoy being lulled to sleep with some soothing refrain, as Webster says.

Birds wake us up—birds, or the garbage truck, or the steady pounding of joggers up and down the street, or the neighbor's lawn mower in summer, or the toot of a horn for the early car pool pick-up.

But what puts us to sleep—in bed, I mean? Crickets, wind sighs, gurgling mountain rivers, whispering pine or palm trees, and the above-mentioned creature comforts for the child in us? Listening to talk shows works wonders for some people, apparently. If it were not so, slumber-set radios wouldn't be such a big-selling item. Actually most of grown-up America counts the ten o'clock news as a bedtime story, with the hype music of sign-off standing in as a lullaby. Small comfort, I say.

What this world needs is a good lullaby for grown-ups. Now, while the lullaby has only been a musical form since the sixteenth century (at least as far as many music historians can discern), it wasn't until the last half of the nineteenth century that Brahms helped everybody out by composing his beloved *Weigenlied* or lullaby. But will that do it? Have you listened to the words lately? "Lullaby and goodnight" . . . so far so good. Then comes "with roses bedight, creep into thy bed, there pillow thy head. If God wilt, thou shalt wake when the morning doth bre-e-ak. . . ." Rose thorns for a pillow, and the fear of death if we're out of favor with God? It's enough to keep one awake and trembling until the dawn.

Brahm's melody is lovely, of course. As a matter of fact it is our family favorite, but we have enjoyed la-la-la-ing it most.

I once asked the late Alexander Schreiner for a list of calming classical numbers with which I could stifle my brain waves at bedtime. Alex was a world-famous organist and cautioned that what works for one person may not work for another. Just because a piece of music is slow, quiet, and melodic doesn't guarantee sleep for everyone. The love theme from *Tristan and Isolde*, for example, might lull one person off before its fifth phrase but keep someone else wide-awake listening rapturously. The same is true of the theme from *Cavaleria Rusticana* by Mascagni.

Moonlight Serenade, "Meditations" from *Thaïs, Madame Butterfly, La Bohème,* and Tchaikovsky's *Pathétique* offer a wide range to choose from. However, hymns rated highest with Dr. Schreiner as music to smooth our ragged edges.

During my university days my science of sound class had a private adventure with Dr. Schreiner, who was the graduate assistant for the class at the time. It was our unique opportunity to have this master show us the inner workings of the great organ in the Tabernacle on Temple Square in Salt Lake City. The lecture and the actual scrutiny of which pipes and reeds made which sounds and why was fascinating. But it was his demonstration at the console that was unforgettable. To hear Dr. Schreiner play Brahms's Lullaby on the organ, with variations on the theme, was a musical privilege. He did that with a familiar hymn, too, playing the theme again and again, changing the organ stops and thus changing the musical experience.

Although Dr. Schreiner was an acclaimed artist at the organ, he had a philosophy of service to mankind in later years that came before his desire to demonstrate organ technique. "People have emotional needs that I enjoy satisfying at the organ." We watched that happen when he did just that for President Richard Nixon and his family when they made a visit to Salt Lake City.

Speaking of music from Temple Square, I became a fan of the Mormon Youth Symphony and Chorus when I gave the spoken word and they presented the musical portion of national broadcasts for a period of several years. Robert C.

Bowden directed the group in a selection of music that works wonders for me when I'm hankering for a soothing mood—while I write or get ready for rest. The recording is entitled *O Divine Redeemer*, and includes gentle renderings of such old favorites as the title song, "The Rugged Cross," "The Lord's Prayer," "Ave Maria," and "Bless This House."

Author/lecturer John Gardner was the keynote speaker at a national convention where Win Jardine and I presented a program for the spouses of the delegates. Our presentation was scheduled at a different hour than his, and so I slipped in to hear him. Since then I have read a good bit of Gardner's work. One of his observations stressed that society must learn to honor excellence, even demand it, in every socially accepted human activity. Both humble and exalted activity should be performed with excellence, said Gardner.

It seemed to me that he had "hardening of the categories" about what was exalted and what was humble activity, but nonetheless the point was well made. He said, "An excellent plumber is infinitely more admirable than an incompetent philosopher. The society which scorns excellence in plumbing because it is a humble activity and tolerates shoddiness in philosophy because it is an exalted activity will have neither good plumbing nor good philosophy. Neither its pipes nor its theories will hold water."

I feel the same way about churches and their congregational singing. You can make an accurate assessment of a church and the level of spirituality of its membership by their congregational singing—not the choir numbers, but how the congregation takes its turn with the hymns. Listless singing indicates to me, at least, that neither the church nor its teachings spurs spirit.

I was interested in a television special about the unprecedented growth in church attendance in Poland since permission has been granted for the rebuilding of Poland's churches. The camera showed full churches, it's true, but the congregational singing was passive. No rousing of the spirit with hearty hymns, no tender turns for diminishing the pain and poverty.

Poland has been sorely assaulted by its enemies for many years, and so its population is overwhelming young in age. That may be an explanation. Still, fervor, or at least attentive singing, reveals the heart and mind of the worshippers. Perhaps there will come a day when the Poles can go to sleep in peace, and then they will feel like singing heartily in church. But I get the feeling that they haven't sung hymns in their homes much either. And that is a sadness to me.

People in Germany worship God and sing of their beliefs with gusto. They are music-bound, of course. To that race we owe our deep debt for Brahms and his lullaby and Franz Gruber and his lullaby, ''Silent Night.'' But have you heard the Germans—not their choirs, but their congregations—sing hymn no. 252 in their native tongue? It is anything but a lullaby! Florence Jacobsen, Bishop Carl Buehner, and I did a Church tour in Europe, and in each of five German cities the musical director chose his hymn, ''Put Your Shoulder to the Wheel'' for congregational singing. ''Stemmt die Schulter an das Rad, frisch und fra-a-nk!'' By the last city, when this hymn popped up one more time, we were hard pressed to stifle giggles—not at the singing, surely, but because of the repetition. We who had traveled so much seemed to have made no progress.

Hymn singing and hymn memorizing enhance peace of mind. Hymn singing is a strong force against temptation, a good reminder of values, and provides the comfort of thinking upon the Savior as a benediction to the day. What better way to recall precious feelings in life than with a lullaby/hymn?

Now the Day Is Over

Calmly ♩ = 60-72

1. Now the day is o - ver; Night is draw-ing nigh;
2. Je - sus, give the wea - ry Calm and sweet re - pose;

Shad - ows of the eve - ning Steal a - cross the sky.
With thy ten-d'rest bless - ing May our eye - lids close.

Text: Sabine Baring-Gould, 1834-1924
Music: Joseph Barnby, 1838-1896

Proverbs 3:24
Alma 37:37

I Need Thee Every Hour

Fervently ♩ = 60-72

1. I need thee ev - ery hour, Most gra - cious Lord.
2. I need thee ev - ery hour; Stay thou near - by.
3. I need thee ev - ery hour, In joy or pain.
4. I need thee ev - ery hour, Most ho - ly One.

No ten - der voice like thine Can peace af - ford.
Temp - ta - tions lose their pow'r When thou art nigh.
Come quick - ly and a - bide, Or life is vain.
Oh, make me thine in - deed, Thou bless - ed Son!

I need thee, oh, I need thee; Ev - ery hour I need thee!

Oh, bless me now, my Sav - ior; I come to thee!

Text: Annie S. Hawkes, 1835-1918
Music: Robert Lowry, 1826-1899

2 Nephi 4:16-35
Psalm 143:1

How Gentle God's Commands

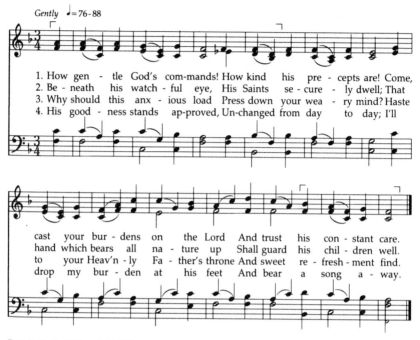

Gently ♩ = 76-88

1. How gen - tle God's com-mands! How kind his pre - cepts are! Come,
2. Be - neath his watch - ful eye, His Saints se - cure - ly dwell; That
3. Why should this anx - ious load Press down your wea - ry mind? Haste
4. His good - ness stands ap-proved, Un-changed from day to day; I'll

cast your bur - dens on the Lord And trust his con - stant care.
hand which bears all na - ture up Shall guard his chil - dren well.
to your Heav'n - ly Fa - ther's throne And sweet re - fresh - ment find.
drop my bur - den at his feet And bear a song a - way.

Text: Philip Doddridge, 1702-1751
Music: Johann G. Nägeli, 1773-1836; arr. by Lowell Mason, 1792-1872

1 John 5:3
Psalm 55:22

Jesus, the Very Thought of Thee

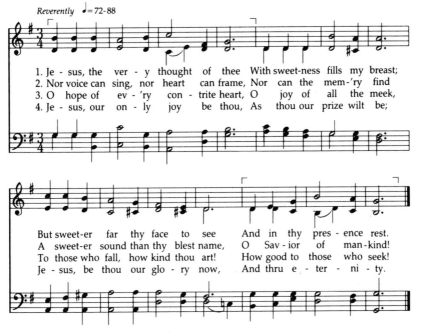

1. Je - sus, the ver - y thought of thee With sweet-ness fills my breast;
2. Nor voice can sing, nor heart can frame, Nor can the mem-'ry find
3. O hope of ev - 'ry con - trite heart, O joy of all the meek,
4. Je - sus, our on - ly joy be thou, As thou our prize wilt be;

But sweet-er far thy face to see And in thy pres - ence rest.
A sweet-er sound than thy blest name, O Sav - ior of man - kind!
To those who fall, how kind thou art! How good to those who seek!
Je - sus, be thou our glo - ry now, And thru e - ter - ni - ty.

Text: Attr. to Bernard of Clairvaux, ca. 1091-1153

Music: John B. Dykes, 1823-1876

Psalm 104:34
Enos 1:27

Where Can I Turn for Peace?

Thoughtfully ♩=80-100

1. Where can I turn for peace? Where is my so - lace
2. Where, when my ach-ing grows, Where, when I lan - guish,
3. He an-swers pri-vate-ly, Reach - es my reach - ing

When oth - er sourc-es cease to make me whole?
Where, in my need to know, where can I run?
In my Geth - sem - a - ne, Sav - ior and Friend.

When with a wound-ed heart, an - ger, or mal - ice,
Where is the qui - et hand to calm my an - guish?
Gen - tle the peace he finds for my be - seech - ing.

I draw my - self a - part, Search - ing my soul?
Who, who can un - der - stand? He, on - ly One.
Con - stant he is and kind, Love with - out end.

Text: Emma Lou Thayne, b. 1924. © 1973 LDS
Music: Joleen G. Meredith, b. 1935. © 1973 LDS

John 14:27; 16:33
Hebrews 4:14-16

Singing a certain song can tighten the years, linking youth with age in a flash of melody. My husband had an accident on ice and suffered a concussion that required stitches in his head and bed rest for healing. It was unprecedented for the children to see their six-foot-six father stretched out and stricken. The three-year-old was devoted in his attention. With his sturdy little body bent forward, Levi's-clad bottom poking out above struggling legs, he'd push a chair over to the bedside each day. He'd climb up on it and begin his round of songs. He had quite a repertoire that included "Home on the Range," "Jesus Wants Me for a Sunbeam," "I Hope They Call Me on a Mission," and "I've Been Working on the Railroad." Sometimes I helped bring smiles myself with my rendition of "In Our Lovely Deseret," with its well-remembered counsel learned in my childhood about despising tea and coffee.

Sometimes the best lullabies aren't lullabies at all.

My husband was a self-employed businessman and a consumed bishop when our children were growing up. His best contribution to family life, and to me as a frazzled mother, was to take out his old Hawaiian ukelele and sit in the hall connecting the bedrooms and the "girls' dorm" to serenade the little destroying angels who had just been tucked in. From his mission days he would sing "Imi Au Ia Oe" and "Across the Sea an Island's Calling Me." Other big favorites were "Casey Jones" and "Ivan Skavinsky Skvar."

We planned a full family reunion to celebrate our forty years as a family. Each of the children, now gone from home, was assigned to write his or her memories of family life. Now, I had cooked, sewn, taxied, bandaged, nursed, staged fabulous birthday parties, and made one million cookies for room parties, planned toilet paper surprises for the high school athletes, and made apologies to the family whose window got broken. I had played Santa and the tooth fairy, and dispenser of wisdom and solace over the many years and over the many children. Who cared? Nobody. How do I know? Because what did the grown-up darlings remember best when they were asked to share their memories for the anniversary? Of course, it wasn't the slave labor of Mother, it was the tenderness of Dad's serenades as he sat on a stool in the hall singing them to sleep.

But such a nice memory.

When our son Tony was fighting for his life, he was a sophomore in high school. His condition had worsened and he felt certain that he was going to die. He had a last request and he got it. His four sisters, Carla, Christine, Susan, and Holly, rearranged their lives to present a command performance in his hospital room. They had sung in close harmony since they could open their mouths; each one in turn had been added to the duet, or trio, or quartet as soon as she learned to talk. Carrying a tune was doing what came naturally to those four. They were professionals in their own way, but singing for "little brother" was a very grown-up, tough experience for them. It was like having a healing blessing for him. When they finished, he turned over and went to sleep for the best rest he had had in weeks. It was a turning point for the better.

One couple struggled with disagreements through their early years of marriage. Their interaction was lively, to say the least. But their attraction for each other and their commitment to sacred covenants kept them hanging on and trying. Then one night the husband sang a gentle little song to his wife when she went to bed sulking and without their usual bedtime prayer together. It worked like magic. Her heart was softened, hugs and kisses happened, and a new system for solving problems began—singing it away.

He sang the old primary song: "If you chance to meet a frown . . ." He sang it with actions, he sang it with strokes upon her hair and her shoulders and on her back, which was turned toward him. He sang it with a deep voice and with a high, childish lilt. He sang it as a funeral dirge and as a sunshine-spreader. He sang it until she responded.

Conrad Aiken wrote some lines I love: ''Music I heard with you was more than music, and bread I broke with you was more than bread.'' It's amazing how that applies in more situations than only with lovers.

For example, my husband and I were cruising the Mississippi River on the luxurious Mississippi Queen when a wonderful sharing of nighttime music was more than music for me.

These flat-bottomed, waterwheel steamboats can pull to shore anyplace along the river. Each cabin has its own private deck on the outside. We had gone to bed when we heard faint singing of ''Goodnight, Ladies'' coming through the open door to the deck. I got up and then beckoned my husband: ''A wonderful thing is happening!''

I explained that there were citizens from a small community on the banks of the mighty Mississippi (my earliest recollection of a grade-school spelling word!) serenading us from shore. We leaned over the railing of our deck to see the serenaders. Others up above, below, and alongside us on the ship were doing the same.

You see, even today when a riverboat banks, the townspeople gather to watch. That night, perhaps because of the late hour, the full moon, the glamorous boat, and their own big American hearts, they sang to us strangers near their shores.

It *was* a wonderful thing.

But that wasn't all.

We were rooming next door to Jeff and Pat Holland, and the four of us took up the lullaby as others on board quickly joined us. We sang ''I Am a Child of God'' in good Mormon harmony. The shore folks loved it and shouted ''More!'' We sang about springtime in the Rockies and about that long, long trail a-winding. They sang "Old Man River." We sang "Let Us All Press On."

Things were getting more wonderful by the time we blended voices to welcome the moon over the Missouri (instead of Miami). Then together we sang "America the Beautiful" and ended the neighborly concert with a joint rendition of "Now the Day Is Over."

Through no stretch of the imagination can these tunes be classified as lullabies, but they worked the magic of music at bedtime.

"O long sweet song . . . ," music more than music!

People can solve their problems with music they've learned. You may have heard how J. Golden Kimball and Heber J. Grant solved theirs.

Heber J. Grant was an enthusiastic singer—not necessarily good, but enthusiastic. His voice carried above the congregation in the Tabernacle at general conference in Salt Lake City, Utah.

He took a trip with J. Golden Kimball once and had a bit of a problem. Brother Grant was not getting enough sleep. They were sharing a room to save money, and J. Golden snored. In fact, J. Golden was famous for snoring.

J. Golden Kimball was as famous for snoring as Heber J. Grant was for singing. Well, one night, hard-pressed for a good night's sleep, Heber J. said to J. Golden, "Brother Kimball, I have purchased some tape and I'd be much obliged if you would wear a piece of it over your mouth tonight. That way I can get some rest. I am sorry, but I am weary of your snoring."

So J. Golden Kimball, the man who snored at night, replied to Heber J. Grant, the man who sang loudly every verse of every song in every meeting: "Certainly, Brother Grant. I'll wear this tape all night if *you will wear it all day!*"

"Fine, brother," said Heber J. Grant. "Now let's sing four verses of 'Master, the Tempest Is Raging!' before we turn in."

"But Brother Grant, there are only three verses in that hymn."

"Well, then, we'll sing the last verse twice."

One of my favorite stories about lullabies I learned as a teenager. I recall the occasion clearly—with whom I was sitting and with whom I was *not* sitting. I recall clearly, too, where *he* was sitting and with whom. I was miserable, and so I listened to the speaker intently.

The youth fireside speaker was LeGrand Richards, Presiding Bishop of the Church at that time. We grew up in an era when parents, teachers, and leaders pounded into our heads: "Success!" "Achievement!" "Personal Progress!" "Increase Your Talents!"

Bishop Richards was different in the way he handled the philosophy of the day. He was a man with talent and a zest for life, and he had the gift of God in him. He also had a rare sense of humor.

The truth he spoke, I remembered. That evening he told us that when he was a mission president he counseled his missionaries that as they were released to go back home they should look the girls over carefully first before settling on one to marry.

"Find one who can do something!" he said. "A man can't just look at a pretty face for the rest of his life."

Everything went along fine with his counsel to the boys, Bishop Richards said, until some years had passed and he became a General Authority, traveling across the Church as a spiritual leader. Following one meeting a man came up to him and said: "President Richards, I was one of your missionaries in the southern states. I have a report I want to make to you."

"Fine. What is your report, son?"

"Well, you may recall how you told us to go home and find a girl who could do something—paint, recite the scriptures, play an instrument?"

"Yes, I recall. I still adhere to that view," replied Bishop Richards.

"Well, sir," the young man continued, "I want you to know that I did that. Just like you said, I went home and checked out the girls. And I found one who could sing!"

"Good! Good for you, lad!"

"Yes. Well, there was one problem. The morning after we were married, I woke up first. When I turned over and looked at her head on the pillow beside me, I was sick! I was really horrified! I kept knocking my hand on my head and muttering, 'Leo, what have you done? Old fellow, what have you gone and done? You character! What *have* you done for time and all eternity?' "

"Yes, yes, son, go on."

"Well, I came up with an idea, so I poked her hard with my elbow to wake her up and I said: 'Sing! Sing for me, will you?' "

"And. . . ."

"Now she sings me to sleep—first—every night."

When Harold B. Lee was newly ordained as President of the Church, he agreed to speak before thousands of college-age people gathered together from the state of Arizona. My group had arranged this Student Association meeting, and it set a record attendance. There hadn't been a prophet in Arizona for thirteen years. It was an unusually fine experience. Successful in every way.

As the group in charge of the event went back to the hotel with President and Sister Lee, we discovered that our accommodations were close on the same floor. We stood visiting with the Lees for a few moments before going to our rooms for the night.

I was exuberant about the experience and the response of the young people. My gratitude for the efforts of this great man to be part of it spilled over into my outburst in the hotel hall.

"If only we could thank you adequately, President Lee!" My mind had been racing for a way to express our appreciation. Then I blurted out: "I know, Tom [Pyke], will you sing our gratitude? Sing "We Thank Thee, O God for a Prophet" or "Bless This House" or whatever, but sing, Tom, sing!"

President Lee was touched but practical. "Elaine, we can't very well have Tom do that. With his great voice he'd have the whole building out of bed." I thought he was going to tell us to forget that idea. Instead, he continued, "Let's go into our room and have him sing there."

We crowded into the Lees' room—not a large group, but too large for the chairs in a commercial hotel room. We sat at the feet of our leader and listened to Tom sing solo, and then we joined with Tom in singing "Did You Think to Pray?" After we finished that hymn we were further blessed to be informally and powerfully taught by President Lee.

That brief period generated a sleepless night of pondering for me. And I wouldn't have traded it for all the sound-sleep nights in history.

Sometimes it is simply better to stay awake and enjoy our blessings.

But if you want to sleep, try singing yourself a lullaby.

To my knowledge, these words written by Robert Louis Stevenson have not been put to music. What a lullaby that would be! But I include it here as a kind of tuneless lullaby, a spoken song of praise and prayer suitable to share the last thing at night:

Lord, behold our family here assembled. We thank Thee for this place in which we dwell; for the love that unites us; for the peace accorded us this day; for the hope with which we expect the morrow; for the health, the work, the food, and the bright skies that make our lives delightful; for our friends in all parts of the earth, and our friendly helpers in this foreign isle. . . . Give us courage, gaiety, and the quiet mind. Spare to us our friends, soften to us our enemies. Bless us, if it may be, in all our innocent endeavors. If it may not, give us strength to encounter that which is to come, that we be brave in peril, constant in tribulation, temperate in wrath, and in all changes of fortune and down to the gates of death, loyal and loving one to another. Amen.

And such is my prayer for you. Goodnight.

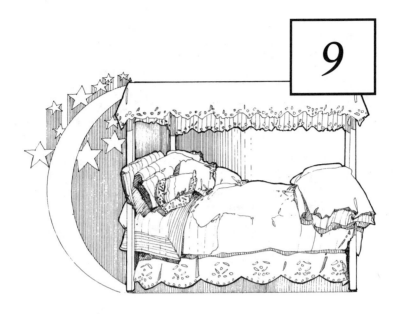

Rest in Peace

Did you hear about the epitaph for an Atheist? Here lies an Atheist—all dressed up with no place to go.

It seems that most little children in my day were taught this comforting prayer to begin a nighttime visit with Heavenly Father:

Now I lay me down to sleep.
I pray Thee, Lord, my soul to keep.
If I should die before I wake,
I pray Thee, Lord, my soul to take.

Once that was recited, then the list of things and people to be thankful for unfolded. Last, one asked for special blessings, ending with a plea to "help me be a good girl!"

In the meantime, I have not only grown up but I have also grown older. The closer I get to the Gate, the more fervent is my hope that I have, indeed, been a good girl. Confidence about that makes one's chances for a good night's rest all the better.

And it's not a bad little verse to begin a bedtime prayer with when one is grown up. Sleep comes easier with the remembrance of God. No matter, he will take care of us.

Sleep is, after all, the brother of death.

I like what Joseph Addison has said about resting in peace:

When I look upon the tombs of the great, every emotion of envy dies in me; when I read the epitaphs of the beautiful, every inordinate desire goes out; when I meet with the grief of parents upon a tombstone, my heart melts with compassion; when I see the tomb of the parents themselves, I consider the vanity of grieving for those whom we must quickly follow: when I see kings lying by those who deposed them, when I consider rival wits placed side by side, or the holy men that divided the world with their contests and disputes, I reflect with sorrow and astonishment on the little competitions, factions, and debates of mankind. When I read the several dates of the tombs, of some that died yesterday, and some six hundred years ago, I consider that great Day when we shall all of us be contemporaries, and make our appearance together.

I read that Addison quote again while standing in Westminster Abbey. Addison had said it well. It was sobering.

But then, knowing what I know of God and his plan, I lifted my eyes from the marked marble beneath my feet to heaven, where pointed the spires of the Abbey. I had paid silent respect before the tombs of the gifted, resting among royalty, but now I praised God. ''How great thou art, O God! And of all thy creations, how wondrous is man! What remarkable souls have peopled the earth! The variety of gifts endowed by thee for music, art, the written word, the interpreted lines, the brave stands, the kindly deeds, the personal sacrifice, the work, the waiting.''

One of the fascinating studies to pursue is how people come to rest in peace. Take Will Rogers. Will was the beloved comedian who helped America see the bright side during the Depression. On one occasion, however, he received a critical letter questioning the example he was setting by playing a certain part in a stage play. It hurt him and started him thinking. As a result, he resigned from the cast and accepted an invitation to fly with Wiley Post around the world in 1935. There was a crash and both men were killed. America still hasn't gotten over it. Will was irreplaceable, even during good times.

Your school days, no doubt, taught you about Aeschylus and the freak accident that took his life. He was killed by the fall of a tortoise, which was dropped on his bald head from the claws of an eagle in the air.

Bacon, it is said, was out in the snow, piling the cold stuff into a large fowl to discern if by this means the meat would ''keep.'' Resourceful, in that day, but nonetheless, he contracted a cold and died.

Robert Burton was the author of *The Anatomy of Melancholy*, and at one stage he astrologically predicted the very day of his own death. And that's when he died!

This one is enough to make you lose your appetite, but legend has it that Fabius, the Roman praetor, was choked by a single goat hair in the milk he was drinking!

When a pig ran under the horse Louis VI was riding, the creature stumbled and horse and rider crashed. It was death for that king. And for another king, death came when he was conducting his queen into a tennis court for a little royal exercise. While stepping through the opening, Charles VIII struck his head on the lintel and he died.

These kinds of details could cause us nightmares . . . "How will I get mine?" for example.

Allen Drury's novels have kept many a reader from sleep over the years—yet another page, another chapter, before turning out the light. In *A Shade of Difference* there is this touching scene about resting in peace:

> The last brisk nurse had popped in with orange juice . . . silence had fallen at last upon the great hospital—and there descended upon him at once the most completely devastating feeling of depression he had ever known. . . . Out of his despair he cried out to a God who had apparently forsaken him, in stumbling words and half-formed phrases that made little sense save agony as he whispered them into the darkened room. . . .
>
> So passed time, how much he did not know, as the long night deepened and with it his awful loneliness. There came the moment eventually when the last defense, a great bitter rage, welled up and he told God that he no longer believed in Him, that He did not exist, that He was a mockery, that no Deity Who could visit upon a man so many pointless agonies could possibly make claim to further faith or respect. And after that, in due course, out of the shattering silence of the universe that followed his anguished repudiation, there came the slow, steady, inevitable restoration of faith; the benison of a

great humility; the knowledge implanted in him in childhood and never far from his thoughts in all his troubles, that God was with him always and that no rejection, however bitter, however violent, however terrible, could remove His loving presence or drive It from the world.

And with this, finally, there came the beginnings of peace; the tentative, struggling, but ever-stronger return of serenity; the gradual regrowth of certitude and hope; the acceptance that passeth understanding, out of the love that passeth understanding. Gradually he stopped raging, stopped crying, stopped worrying, stopped forever being torn apart by alternatives and might-have-beens. For reasons he could not understand, for purposes not of his own making, he had been given a path to follow in his closing days on earth: So be it. Thus had the Lord directed him, and thus would he do. Never again in the time remaining would he be a victim to doubt and despair. So God was not mad at him, and though he did not understand God's reasons, he would believe in them and go forward in the calm certainty that, in some way he perhaps would never understand, they made sense and would give him strength to do . . . whatever.

It was thus with a growing serenity and peace that he heard the phone ring and, lifting the receiver, heard a quiet voice saying, "Hal, this is Harley. How are you feeling?"

"I'm feeling fine," he said, and there was in his words a vigor and joy that thrilled and startled them both.

"Well, I think that's wonderful," the President said. "Wonderful for you, and wonderful for all of us."

"Harley," Hal asked, still eagerly, and still almost like a little child, a happy child now, wanting to share with someone what had happened to him, "Do you ever have experiences like that, in what you're doing? I mean, when it seems as though there's no way out, and you feel an awful despair and start thinking there isn't any God, and then—all of a sudden, when you've finally told Him you're all through with Him—you suddenly realize He's still there, that He's been there all the time, watching over you just the same as always?"

"Yes, I do," the President said after a moment, when he found he could speak again. "You don't know how often it happens in this office."

"It's a wonderful thing, isn't it?"

"It's a wonderful thing. God bless you, Hal. May you have a good journey and come safe to harbor."

"I will," he said with an eager confidence. "I will."

He lay completely still for perhaps five minutes after their conversation ended. An utter calm, an utter peace flooded into his heart and took gentle dominion of his mind. His exhausted body relaxed. He slept, as deeply and sweetly as a child. (Excerpt from *A Shade of Difference* by Allen Drury. Copyright © 1962 by Allen Drury. Reprinted by permission of Doubleday, a division of Bantam, Doubleday, Dell Publishing Group, Inc.)

Sometimes the Big Sleep can be a laughing matter. For example, Eleanor Donnenfeld and I enjoyed the hour's walk along the waterfront between the convention center and our hotel in Kiel, Germany. We had good times comparing stories about our respective lives. That Jewish girl from New York and this Mormon girl from out in Utah found we had a lot more in common than the International Council of Women meetings.

She told me the following joke. I've told it since, substituting the women of my own cultural background, and it works just as well. This is her version as I remember it:

A chartered plane carrying members of Hadassah back from a pilgrimage to Tel Aviv crashed in the crossing. Once they were in the afterlife, these Jewish girls were found running true to form. They were holding all manner of meetings and benefits. They were stirring up causes and introducing changes. In fact, they had become somewhat of a nuisance, particularly to the authorities, who finally lost their patience, talked to Satan, and asked him to take the ladies of Hadassah off their hands. This he did.

A few days later Satan was on the phone demanding that these women be taken back.

"Why?" he was asked.

"Well, they're ruining everything down here. They've raised enough money to air-condition the place!"

In a great gathering of religious leaders and hooked via modern communication systems to listeners across the world, a speaker repeated an interesting account that had been published in an eastern newspaper. I was in that most attentive audience. Later, letters poured into his office from far places in response. A chord had been struck in many hearts.

There was a fire in the clothing district of New York City. More than a dozen people died—in a cluster—within easy access of an escape door. Because of smoke and fear they had chosen to huddle together and hope for the best, apparently. Or they hadn't known about the door. If only one of the dozen had known of the door, he might have led the others to safety.

Although they had worked in that factory for a period of time, they had either not bothered to learn of safety factors and exits or they had paid little attention to such information if it had been given to them. At any rate, in their hour of crisis, they were not able to find a way out.

It is like so many of us in life. We don't become expert at those truths that would make living easier and more meaningful and death less dreadful.

"Smoke and fear" are all about us. So are light and truth. If you have access to the Book of Mormon, turn to 1 Nephi 12:17–18 and read about the "mists of darkness," which are likened to the temptations of the devil. These blind the eyes and harden the hearts of the children of men, and thus lead them away into "broad roads, that they perish and are lost."

Needless, pitiful death of the spirit.

Faith Precedes the Miracle, by Elder Spencer W. Kimball, might well be a helpful book for anyone suffering from "smoke and fear," or lethargy in finding answers to life and death.

He includes a sermon of sorts based on the principles of truth found in Deuteronomy 8:17–18: "And thou say in thine heart, My power and the might of mine hand hath gotten me this wealth. But thou shalt remember the Lord thy God: for it is he that giveth thee power to get wealth."

Elder Kimball tells of accompanying a friend to the local bank, where the man showed him the rich contents of his safety deposit box—stocks, bonds, deeds, and other treasures. "All these are mine," he said proudly. "These represent the labor of a lifetime."

To himself, Spencer Kimball wondered about the man's attitude: "How you have prospered! How did you do so well? Where did you get your talents, your abilities! Did you create your sight and voice and memory and ability to think? . . . Do you render unto God that which already was his own? I'm sure that Caesar never fails to get his portion. What of God?" . . .

Then Elder Kimball spoke to the man, "By what great power do you earn?"

"My brains," the man replied.

And then Elder Kimball asked the man where he got his brains—did he build them in a factory, or buy them in a store, or did he create them himself along with his soul?

The story ends with this paragraph:

"I outlived this man. . . . It was a sad affair when his time came. The strong was weak, the powerful inanimate. His brains still encased in his cranium would work no more. He breathed no air; he taught no youth, commanded no more hearers, no more salary; he occupied no apartment but did occupy a little plot of earth on a grassy hillside. But now, I hope he knows that "the earth is the Lord's, *and all that therein is.*" (Spencer W. Kimball, *Faith Precedes the Miracle* [Salt Lake City: Deseret Book, 1972], pp. 285–87.)

During a certain period of my life, I traveled to New York City many times with Belle Spafford, one of the great ladies I've known. What fine things to learn from this wise woman and how far-reaching her applications of life's experiences!

There semed to be a theme to her conversations each time we visited, reflecting where her heart was and what her mind was pondering during that period. On one trip she talked about enduring to the end. She knew that she had cancer and that any time it might flare up. Death was a shadow, at the moment, over her productive life. She spoke of visiting with Relief Society women at a retirement home. Following her talk the women expressed their feelings to her.

One said that even though there were meetings right at the "home," she didn't go to church anymore because she didn't think it mattered at her age. Another didn't keep personal standards of avoiding strong beverages. Another didn't pay tithes and offerings to the Church on the basis that God didn't expect it of her anymore. Another complained that a daughter only came to visit because she felt duty-bound to do so—for show. She admitted there was no love shared between them.

Observed Belle: "Sympathetic as we may be toward these sisters and toward their circumstances, and understanding as we may be of their actions, yet we must recognize that with clear minds they were justifying their nonobservance of God's laws. I am led to ask also, Has the Lord ever set a retirement age for keeping his commandments?"

Whenever that last sleep comes for us, may we be ready for it—ready to rest in peace. And until then . . .

Flowers are the fragrant send-off, the tribute of life and the romance of death. Lightly trembling, they speak of gentle times with a loved one who has moved on. Columbine, pale, incredibly fragile and fanciful, barberries so splendid, speak a different message. African daisies of hardy foliage and crisp petals match a mind that dwelt, in its turn, on precise matters like the discipline of children and the righting of adult wrongs —judgment and wisdom softened by good intentions. Tulips are the same, but they do their work of reminding with more elegance. And if they are white, how they rival the rose!

My family and I used a multitude of basic (and therefore handsome) clay pots filled with white tulips, imported to surround the sleeping couch and white mohair throw on our young and well-loved daughter-in-law. It was January, and in our lives as well the year stood at its coldest. Tulips reminded us of the resurrection that a spring will bring.

Goldenrod, statice, and its cousin, heather, regal delphinium—blue is best—announce the dignity of a life. Violets say love was there and innocence—anyway. Cyclamen in pristine beauty, protected by deep-green leafing, suggest that there was a slight withholding of giving, but what a promise of ecstasy in that secluded grouping that rivals orchids!

Hydrangea in great poofs of celebration, and daisies for the sheer delight and eternal youth as well as freshness in life forever—these present death as a gift.

Sleep, remember, is the brother of death. So it is my choice to have flowers by my bedside when I lay me down to sleep each night. The smallest, imperfect, single bloom from the garden will do. A twig of star pine in a cobalt-blue vase . . .

I remember as a young girl in the bloom of my life, being in the hospital at Christmas, with boy friends who brought me flowers and neighbors who sent poinsettia against loneliness in the season. At night it was the nurse's duty to remove the flowers from my bedside to the hall, lest they steal *my* oxygen, she said. (Give me breath and life, is what I'd say.) I'd stay awake and wonder about my flowers, which had come with a price because of those war years. Were they guarding my door, or had they been swept away by the maintenance crew, or taken home from their public place? But each morning they were come again, those flowers used to softly guard against intrusion and to signify that someone loved is close.

Flowers at funerals are the best use of them, then.

There were enormous mounds of flowers at Marie's funeral. And when her grave had been dedicated, Milt asked the mourners (and oh, we mourned that lovely mother of seven and friend to all!) to take the fresh plants and cuttings as a remembrance. They would only freeze in that deepest snowfall of many years, and the plenty left would serve as a blanket on that wintry day.

My husband and I met a new friend at a dinner party in a small town, out of our lifetime orbit. I say friend, for thus we became when the Winstons drew forth each guest, in detail, to hasten understanding. Edith Whithead owned The Garden of Edith and flavored each occasion with her artist's touch in a presentation of fresh flowers. It was her gift to a desert community, heightened by her reverence for life and love of God's creations, her sensitive seeking to make a floral piece that was representative of the bride or the deceased.

Especially the deceased. Edith would lie awake nights and consider what she could ''make up'' in flowers and vines and ribbon to speak of a life well lived, a life raced through, a life that tasted of this and that, or a life narrowed in duty and programmed the same all of its days.

''People don't die when it is convenient,'' Edith explained. So there is considerable sacrifice of personal time to meet death's schedule and to help aching hearts with rosemary sprigs and thistle stems, umbrella tree berries, cactus rose and palm fronds adding a touch of the desert to carnation. Over the years of servicing the community funerals with beauty, Edith made an extravagant hat of flowers for the lady who always wore hats—even to the corner store. There were footballs and musical instruments, a gavel, an open book, and other messages of personality created in flowers.

As an excuse, even as an explanation for actions or attitudes, a friend keeps repeating to me, "But when you are dead, you are dead!"

And I relentlessly respond: "Only for a twinkling of an eye. You pop up to a different tune, that's all." How we are strung here makes all the difference there.

Perhaps it is time now for a little Dickinson to soften sleep, to pacify fears, to express what each of us has felt on occasion:

> My life closed twice before its close;
> It remains to see
> If immortality unveil
> A third event to me,
> So huge, so hopeless to conceive,
> As these that twice befell,
> Parting is all we know of heaven,
> And all we need of hell.

(Emily Dickinson, *My Life Closed Twice*.)

Well, if you aren't asleep yet, how about some other information about the subject of the Big Sleep? The study of wakes, funerals, processionals, viewings, memorials, graveside services, last words of endless perspective about where man has been, and where he's going, and how he's going to get there.

This is absolutely fascinating to some of us. The rest of you, as I have said before, can read along a bit until Nod takes over.

I have taught Shakespeare, and I took classes to learn enough to teach. And one thing I learned is that Shakespeare has a lot to say about death.

Of all the lines to hear about death, listening to Christopher Plummer on Broadway in *Macbeth* is an emotional experience:

> Nothing in his life
> Became him like the leaving it; he died
> As one that had been studied in his death
> To throw away the dearest thing he owed,
> As 'twere a careless trifle.

Once I was involved in building a replica of the Shakespearean theater with its trapdoor for the burial scenes. It was borrowed by schools, churches, ladies' clubs, and finally the Deseret Industries got it!

We got all caught up in the funeral customs of the times, with making a miniature canopy, bier, and royal trappings, or replica rags for commoners in the scripts. We made banners and wax seals. We rendered royal arms. We studied funerals of the Elizabethan period.

Of all the state funerals conducted during the years surrounding Shakespeare's life, historians noted that Queen Elizabeth's processional was the most superb, the most extravagant.

First, all the marshall's men cleared the way, followed by two hundred forty "poor women," walking four-by-four. (I wonder, Were they chosen? Was it an honor to serve or a punishment?)

Then followed the knights, the household servants, the grooms, the musicians, the surgeons, the chief clerks, the porters, the department chiefs, the Lord Keeper of the Great Seal, the agents, the lord Mayors, the bishops, barons, viscounts, and all the lords and ladies, gentlewomen, chamber ladies, and more.

The Archbishop of Canterbury preceded the chariot containing Queen Elizabeth. The body of the queen was in a lead coffin, but there she was on top, in effigy, crowned, and in her robes of parliament. Last of all, after Sir Walter Raleigh, was the famed guard, marching five-by-five with halberds downward.

(I suspect most readers aren't going to leap out of bed and look up the word *halberd*, and few of us would recognize that term without some research. A *halberd*, according to Webster, is a battle-ax and pike mounted on a long pole, measuring at least six feet.)

The multitudes of commoners openly grieved and groaned as the queen's processional passed. When their own time came, commoners were uncoffined and wrapped in a shroud that was tied at each end. Sometimes the face was left exposed. Graves were used over and over, as soon as the decay of body and bones was sufficiently under way. This meant a fairly frequent business of grave-digging to check the corpse.

One more bit of interest. It wasn't until after the sixteenth century that the custom of erecting headstones over graves became the fashion and a person could call his grave his own —a place where he could rest in peace.

What last thing fills the mind of man, of woman, preparing to slip from this to That? Who stands by to hear their words? What is legend? What is truth? We think of last moments with our own loved ones, and things we have heard about the final hours of people we know. . . . *"Find Father, tell him* to come for *me!"* . . . *"Say hello to Marie"* . . . *"But who will deal with the IRS?"*

Family legends.

Great figures in history fascinate collectors of ideas. The last words of some have been published in various forms. I'm including a scant selection just for the fun of it, gathered from several sources.

Benjamin Franklin lay on his death bed. He was being attended by his daughter, who suggested that he might be more comfortable if he changed his position in bed. He could breathe more easily, perhaps.

"A dying man can do nothing easy," replied Franklin. It was the last thing she heard him say.

On the scaffold, in the infamous year of 1793, France's Louis XVI cried out: "May my blood cement your happiness!" This has become a famous phrase in French: *"Puisse mon sang cimenter votre bonheur!"*

"I shall hear in heaven," Beethoven reportedly said. One thinks of the promise made by God to man of the resurrection and of the restoration of all things, and of the hope of the handicapped after proud struggles on earth.

Washington Irving country in New York is a fine tourist haunt. The lore and the memorabilia, the restoration of church and store, the markings of Sleepy Hollow, and other settings familiar to Irving's fans include legends about the man. His last words were worthy of his practical nature, "I must arrange my pillows for another weary night." Sounds like a line from *Rip Van Winkle*.

167

Queen Victoria's husband, lover, and consort, Albert, to whom monuments and honors were heaped to keep his memory alive, said what we all might adopt at death: "I have such sweet thoughts. I have had wealth, rank, and power; but if these were all I had, how wretched I should be!"

"This is the last of earth! I am content," smiled John Quincy Adams, as documented in Josiah Quincy's *Life of John Quincy Adams*.

John Milton said this when he was very much alive, but since it has to do with death, I sum this section with it: "A death-like sleep, a gentle wafting to immortal life."

As for me, I'm with the devoted ornithologist, Alexander Wilson, who said, "Bury me where the birds will sing over my grave."

After death, what? Well, plans for the funeral, for one thing, though many people make arrangements for their own services in connection with writing a will.

Have you yet read *Cold Sassy Tree* by Olive Ann Burns? The Grandpa had written a letter to be read immediately upon his death—no time should be wasted in the doing, and he wanted all his family gathered to hear his instructions. Not a bad idea, it seems to me.

Sometimes those who are entitled to a funeral know better than the survivors what would be comforting and appropriate. I found this letter in this delightful book to be full of ideas at least, and at best wonderful bedtime reading for the very grown up:

Papa walked around to Granny's side of the bed and tore open the envelope.

"Mr. Blakeslee didn't tell me what's in this," he began. "He just said if anything happened to him I was to get the letter out of the safe and read it to y'all right away:"

". . . This is about the disposal of my earthly remains.

". . . Now I want my burying to remind folks that death aint always awful. God invented death. Its in God's plan for it to happen. So when my time comes I don't want no trip to Birdsong's Emporium or any other. Dressing somebody up to look alive don't make it so.

"I dont want no casket. Its a waste of money. What I would really like is to be wrapped in two or three feed sacks and laid right in the ground. But that would bother you all, so use the pine box upstairs at the store that Miss Mattie Lou's coffin come in. I been saving it. And tho I just as soon be planted in the vegetable patch as anywhere, I don't think anybody would ever eat what growed there, after. Anyhow, take me right from home to the cemetery . . . if it is hot weather, my advisement is dont waste no time. Dont put Not Dead But Sleeping on my stone. Write it Dead, Not Sleeping. Being dead under six foot of dirt wont bother me a-tall, but I hate for it to sound like I been buried alive.

"Now then, the funeral party. In case you all aint noticed, the first three letters of the word funeral spells FUN. So a week or two after I die, you all have dinner at the ball park . . . have a happy get-together with kinfolks and old friends. Tell funny stories about me and such. . . . I don't want nobody at the funeral party to wear black or cry either one. Dont go if you cant be pleasant. If you do go, dress up and act happy. You can cry later. . . ." (*Cold Sassy Tree* [New York: Dell, 1984], pp. 380–82.)

In 1980, the second World Conference on Records was held in Salt Lake City, Utah—Alex Haley was the special star.

I was the warm-up act—the prelude speaker, if you will, to keep the people happy who arrived in the great convention center early to get a good seat for the Haley presentation.

It was worth it to me—I earned the best seat in the house! And there was a chance to talk with the man and feel his good spirit.

Mr. Haley is absolutely sure that the ancestors he'd so persistently traced are "up there watchin'." Grandma, Cousin Georgia, who'd told him so many great stories, and all of the others too. There were Kuinta and Bell, Kizzy, Chicken George and Matilda, and so on. And then there was Alex Haley's "Dad."

When Dean Haley died he was eighty-three; his four children planned the funeral, which included remarks from each of them. The casket was left open, and each one would go and stand by the open coffin and tell about "Dad." Writes Alex:

"I got up as George took his seat. . . . Being the oldest child, I could remember things farther back about the gentleman lying there. For instance, my first distinct boyhood impression of love was noticing how Dad's and Mama's eyes would look at each other over the piano top when Mama was playing some little introduction as Dad stood near waiting to sing in our church."

Alex Haley told about the year 1915 when his dad was trying to work his way through college with four part-time jobs. As a train porter, he met a man who later sent a check to the college for the full amount of tuition, books, and lodging, meals included.

Said Haley: "And that was how our dad got his master's degree at Cornell, and then was a professor, so that we, his children . . . , the seventh generation from Kunta Kinte . . . , grew up amid those kinds of influences . . . ; why we were fortunate enough to be there seeing Dad off now with me as an author, George as an assistant director of the United States Information Agency, Julius as a U.S. Navy Department architect, and Lois as a teacher of music." (Alex Haley, *Roots* [Garden City, NY: Doubleday and Company, 1976], p. 688.)

For all of us who love the Lord, the ultimate story of what happens after death is His own story. We are familiar with the heartbreaking but lifting biblical account of the last days of Christ and the first days after the resurrection. But there is another side to the stories that have grown out of this event. There is a treasure of a book published in London and New York by St. Martin's Press called *The Book of Witnesses*. It was written by a Jew who was a successful British actor. It offers a perspective that makes a satisfying bedtime story for grown-ups. The following is a portion of that creative author's viewpoint:

> I'm perfectly willing to tell you all I know about the night the preacher's body went from the tomb, but all I know doesn't amount to very much—and it may be the truth—although those who told me weren't even there.
>
> I get my orders from priests. The Temple Guard are really policemen. Our authority comes from the elders, the Sanhedrin Council, the religious parties.
>
> That's where the order came from that Saturday morning. The offices of High Priest Caiaphas, and the Pharisee Party. The order was simple and clear. A ten-man guard detail with two officers to proceed to the burial ground alongside Crucifixion Hill and mount a day-and-night guard on a tomb. No details given at all as to occupant of the tomb, whose owner was Councillor Joseph of Arimathea, my father's second cousin. Uncle Joseph, who was very much alive.
>
> We were up to the tomb by noon. . . . Two men from Temple maintenance were sealing the front stone with clay—and attaching the official tags. Seemed a needless procedure. . . . somebody—or something—very valuable in there, my corporal said.
>
> We sorted out our roster and settled in. . . . As I say, what did actually happen I can't tell you—mainly because I was asleep. It was just before dawn. . . . What woke me was a mixture of things really. A blinding white

light and men shouting in terror. My men, I'm not proud to tell you. There was a sound like a great wind, and a movement in the ground, like an earthquake—or a landslide. I was dazed. As I tried to get to my feet, my corporal, in full flight, with his eyes staring out of his head, went straight into me.

We both hit the ground together. I caught his fear. I've never been so frightened—or known less why. I felt some great thing was happening, to do with the blinding light and the earth movement. . . . Everything went dark and I fainted! It couldn't have been for long. . . . The great white light had gone. It was a pale dawn.

You know, sometimes you just don't believe what your eyes tell you. The stone had been rolled right back! Right back, as though it weighed a penny. Rolled on edge—like a penny! Not a lever, or a footmark, or a clue of any kind. The tomb was empty—except for some body wrappings. If there had been valuables— they'd gone. (David Kossoff, *The Book of Witnesses*, p. 176.)

Remember Ted Malone and his intimate radio show, where he read nostalgic poetry to a world gone sour through Depression and worldwide war and heartbreak . . . remember? During that period he published collections of thoughts that were tremendously popular, many editions, and boasted introduction by the Director of Poetry of the Library of Congress, no less.

Simple verses for a time when minds and souls were tired of the struggle—good enough for today. Here's one by Dorothy Curran that has a nice ring to it:

> I ask
> But an hour of music
> When I die,
> No service, sermon, prayer,
> Nor sad good-bye.
> It is enough
> That I should go,
> Armed with a song
> Sung soft and low.

Good idea! And since *we all know* where we are going, we may not need to teach our mourners about God through song. So how about some healthy sentiment regarding what we're leaving behind? How about "Auld Lang Syne," or a little Glenn Miller, or "A Wintry Day," or the love theme from *Tristan and Isolde*?

There are certain people whose contribution to our thinking is so overwhelming that we are eternally in their debt. To read the works of Will and Ariel Durant is to love life more, to honor the plan of God as it is seen to unfold through their massive revelations of what has gone on across the centuries. To become familiar with their literary style is to know comfort from beauty, even if the subject is distressing.

To the Durants, history is "an encouraging remembrance of generative souls." They are generative souls. This perspective on death is taken from their small book called *The Lessons of History*, and it gives a perspective on death quite different from what we usually get:

> Death is natural, and if it comes in due time it is forgivable and useful, and the mature mind will take no offense from its coming. But do civilizations die? . . . not quite. Greek civilization is not really dead; only its frame is gone and its habitat has changed and spread; it survives in the memory of the race, and in such abundance that no one life, however full and long, could absorb it all. Homer has more readers now than in his own day and land. . . .
>
> Nations die. Old regions grow arid, or suffer other change. Resilient man picks up his tools and his arts, and moves on, taking his memories with him. . . .
>
> As life overrides death with reproduction, so an aging culture hands its patrimony down to its heirs across the years and the seas. Even as these lines are being written, commerce and print, wires and waves and invisible Mercuries of the air are binding nations and civilizations together, preserving for all what each

has given to the heritage of mankind. (Will and Ariel Durant, *The Lessons of History* [New York: Simon and Schuster, 1968], pp. 93–94. Copyright © 1968 by Will and Ariel Durant; reprinted by permission of Simon and Schuster, Inc.)

Sleepy? Good! And peaceful rest, knowing that life goes on, even while we sleep.
''Now I lay me down . . . ''

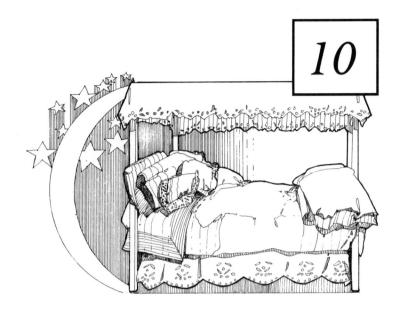

And After a Good Night . . .

Assuming that you finally get to sleep, the next thing you know is that the morning breaks and shadows flee. After a good night, what then?

Well, the world out there is waiting for you. Can you face the day?

How about some A.M. exercises? Ready?

Up . . . down . . . up . . . down . . . up . . . down.

Now the other lid!